The
Leverage
EQUATION

The Leverage Equation: How to Work Less, Make More, and Cut 30 Years Off Your Retirement Plan

Todd Tresidder

Copyright © 2018 | Todd R. Tresidder

Published by FinancialMentor.com

ISBN for Print 978-1-939273-02-4

ISBN for Ebook 978-1-939273-03-1

Financial Mentor and the Financial Mentor logo are trademarks or registered trademarks of CreateCorp Business Solutions, Inc. and/or its affiliates, in the United States and other countries, and may not be used without written permission. All other trademarks are the property of their respective owners.

For bulk orders, please contact todd@financialmentor.com for a generous discount schedule.

The
Leverage
EQUATION

How to Work Less, Make More, and
Cut 30 Years Off Your Retirement Plan

TODD TRESIDDER

FinancialMentor©
Financial Freedom for Smart People.

To my wife, Katherine,
and our wonderful daughters,
Jenna and Ashley.

Thank you for your patience and support.
Every word was written with you in my mind.

LIMIT OF LIABILITY
DISCLAIMER OF WARRANTY

was written and when it was read. While every effort has been made to make this book as complete and accurate as possible, there may be mistakes, both typographical and in content. Use at your own risk.

ADDITIONAL BOOKS
BY TODD TRESIDDER

How Much Money Do I Need To Retire?

Don't Hire a Financial Coach!
(Until You Read This Book)

The 4% Rule and Safe Withdrawal Rates in Retirement

Variable Annuity Pros and Cons:
Surprising Truths Your Advisor Won't Tell You

Investment Fraud:
How Financial "Experts" Rip You Off
and What To Do About It

ADDITIONAL COURSES
BY TODD TRESIDDER

Expectancy Wealth Planning

Risk Management:
How To Make More By Risking Less

CONTENTS

─────────── STRATEGIES ───────────

IMPLEMENTATION

OVERVIEW

INTRODUCTION

How can you lift a 7000-pound car without anyone to help you?

The answer is the same as how you can achieve financial independence well before your retirement age. It's the same solution that will get more done in a day, with less effort. And it's the answer to breaking free of almost any limitation you think you have – whether it's time, money, skills, connections, or anything else.

Leverage is the strategic tool that expands your resources beyond your present limitations to produce greater results than you could generate on your own. Leverage gives you access to more capital, more technology, larger networks, greater knowledge, and smarter systems than you personally possess.

Mastering leverage can:

- Accelerate your financial results
- Multiply your wealth

- Improve your quality of life by freeing up your time from mundane tasks
- Allow you to focus your attention on what you enjoy and are good at

Mastering leverage is how I retired at age 35, just 12 years after graduating from college with thousands of dollars in student loan debt and zero assets. In this book, you'll discover how to apply the same leverage principles I used (and more!) to break through whatever limitations hold you back so you can produce even greater results.

THE DECEPTIVE HALF-TRUTHS THAT HOLD YOU BACK

Most people misunderstand leverage.

For example, when you hear the term "leverage" do you think of financial leverage, such as mortgages in real estate or debt financing?

Sure, that's one type of leverage, but it's only one of six! It's also the riskiest. The other five types of leverage multiply reward *without* increasing risk. Even better, when you master certain types of leverage, it's entirely possible to increase your reward while reducing your risk at the same time!

Another common myth about leverage is that it's exploitative or manipulative. Maybe you've seen the depraved villain on a daytime soap "use" people through leverage in some shocking and morally bankrupt way. You think: "I would never do a thing like that!"

But leverage is not about "using" people. It's about making smart business decisions that benefit all participants; and it's about responsibly applying other people's resources to overcome obstacles that limit your success so you can achieve greater results with less personal effort. Leverage done right creates jobs, grows wealth, and serves people.

THE 4 PIECES OF CONVENTIONAL WISDOM I DON'T ENDORSE IN THIS BOOK

There's plenty of success advice out there. Unfortunately, many of the ideas taught are really just conditional half-truths masquerading as universal facts. The problem is: these half-truths frequently work well and are repeated so often that it's easy to accept them as fact. But that's where the danger begins, because any idea taken as fact – when it actually isn't – will limit your ability to see better alternatives. You won't recognize the exceptions that disprove the rule.

The good news is that when you learn the pros and cons of the multiple leverage strategies taught in this book, you'll see how much of the conventional "wisdom" is really just low-leverage half-truths.

For example:

1.   Retirement planning is NOT just about saving and investing until age 65 (Spoiler alert: You can become financially independent at any age! You don't have to wait until age 65; leverage will show you how to enjoy financial freedom earlier).

2.   Asset allocation across a diversified portfolio of stocks, bonds, and mutual funds is NOT the only way to invest for retirement (Spoiler alert: Higher leverage asset classes and investment models exist that can accelerate your wealth while reducing your risk).

3.   Making more money is NOT just about getting a promotion, or a raise, or working longer hours (Spoiler alert: trading time for money caps your income because there's a limit to how many hours you can work. You must learn how to separate your income from hours worked so you can make more while working less).

4.   It does NOT take money to make money (Spoiler alert: you can separate your wealth growth from your return on equity equation by leveraging other assets).

Don't worry if you have subscribed to any of these conventional beliefs about investing and wealth *before* reading this book. It's not your fault. They're repeated so often by mainstream media that it's easy for your mind to accept them as true without questioning their validity.

This book will open your mind to different strategies for achieving success and breaking through the roadblocks that hold you back. You'll discover a new framework built on leverage that will unlock these mental traps. It will open the door to a completely different way of producing greater results with less effort and using fewer of your own resources (including time and money).

This isn't get-rich-quick hype. It's a provable fact based on financial science, rooted in research, and grounded in mathematics (but don't worry – it's just high school algebra). The point is that it's real, and I'll show you *exactly* how it works.

Not only that; it's common sense. You already know it's true because the evidence is all around you. For example, when you hear in the news how someone went from zero to multi-millionaire by age 20 or 30, what was the mechanism? How did they do it?

With the rare exception of extreme frugality at an early age, every one of those stories involves either business or real estate success. That's because these two asset classes offer multiple opportunities for leverage so wealth can be created more quickly than investing through conventional asset allocation.

In fact, the research on how the rich get that way proves that the vast majority of wealth is created through business entrepreneurship and real estate. Conventional paper asset investing through stocks, bonds, and mutual funds takes a distant third place, and even then it's usually after an entire lifetime of saving and compounding.

So if conventional paper asset investing is the slowest strategy for wealth building, why do financial experts promote it? Because it's a one-size-fits-all solution that's easy to *sell* and it has the backing of academic research proving its validity. It's a good business model for the investment firms – because it's simple to communicate and implement; because it's generic and doesn't require them to develop a plan that accounts for your personal strengths; and because it doesn't require any special adaptation to your timeline or personal goals. It's an efficient business model for *them*, but it's not the most effective alternative for *you*. It's not wrong, but there are faster, more efficient ways to grow your wealth that may match your life situation and goals much better.

If you want financial independence while you're still young enough to enjoy it, and without being dependent on extreme frugality to make the numbers work; or if you would like to use alternative asset classes like business or real estate in your wealth plan; then you'll want to broaden your thinking by trying strategies that are different from the generic financial advice you get everywhere else.

Either you'll learn to master leverage or you'll work far harder than necessary to produce far fewer results than you're capable of. This book, *The Leverage Equation: How to Work Less, Make More, and Cut 30 Years off Your Retirement Plan* – will help you completely shift your awareness. It will give you the essential tools that you need to work smarter – not harder – in order to achieve tangible results in your financial life.

By the end of this book, you'll know:

- The real reason you're not as rich as you should be (Surprise! It's not what you think…)

- How $10 can realistically become $1000 (without taking crazy risk or working long hours)

- The hidden trap of regular paychecks (and how you can overcome it!)

- The truth about (and the dangers of!) highly leveraged investments

- The 9 principles of leverage that maximize your financial results (and lead to a more fulfilling life)

- The right (and wrong) way to apply each of the six types of leverage.

Plus, you'll get more than 100 practical, usable examples of leverage strategies that you can implement immediately in your business and financial plans. (In fact, you can download the full list of *"101 Leverage Hacks: A Cheat Sheet for Quickly Implementing Leverage in Your Wealth Plan"* right now at https://financialmentor.com/free-stuff/leverage-book)

YOU'RE ALREADY A MASTER OF LEVERAGE

Best of all, you're already a master of leverage because you use it *every day*. It's not technical or complex. In fact, it's so common that you don't even realize you're using it, and that's why you haven't yet consciously put it to work to grow your wealth and improve your life.

For example, every day you're already leveraging:

- All the employees who manufacture the cars you drive (but that you didn't build).

- The workers who created the clothes you wear – from the seamstress who sewed the item, to the textile company that created the fabric, to the farmer who grew the raw material.

- Your smartphone, which you use to accomplish many tasks – and that leverage extends beyond the functionality built into the phone to include the electricity you use to charge it and the engineering talent that designed it.

The fact is you're already leveraging other people's skills and resources almost every minute of your life. Leverage is an automatic part of your day. The difference is it's just not conscious; that is, it's not conscious until something breaks.

A few years ago, I was skiing when a massive storm knocked down a major power line, cutting off all power to the town and surrounding area. There was no electricity, so almost nothing worked; the cell phone towers went out, and the airport only functioned because of backup generators.

Just imagine being stuck in a freezing house in a massive storm with no electricity, no heat, no lights, no cooking, and no phone or data connectivity – and you'll begin to understand how leverage-dependent our lives have become. Then imagine no running water as well, because, in this case, they had to drain the system to protect the pipes from freezing. That means no toilets, no showers, no drinking water, no heat, no electricity, etc.

None of these resources belonged to *me*. On this trip, I was leveraging all of them for my own use – until they stopped working. It was a wake-up call, because the reality is that nearly every aspect of our lives is touched by leverage in some form in order to increase quality and efficiency. Leverage generally operates so smoothly that we scarcely even notice it's happening.

But there is a big difference in how the people who become wealthy use leverage – and that's what this book will show you. *They're intentional and strategic in how they apply it.* They use it to accelerate results in their wealth plans.

With *The Leverage Equation*, you too will learn how to take your casual, everyday use of leverage and repurpose it into a deliberate, strategic, wealth-building strategy.

You'll become a master of using – in uncommon ways

— what is all around you every day, in order to produce much greater results with much less effort.

APPLYING LEVERAGE IN YOUR LIFE

As you begin this exciting journey, always remember that *nobody* gets rich without leverage. If you aren't employing leverage in your business and wealth plans, it means you're compromising the speed, time, and work effort necessary to reach each level of success.

Leverage isn't difficult to master; it's something you can implement right away and then reap the benefits for years to come.

It's time for you to stop working harder than you *should* to earn less than you *could*. Leverage will show you how to break the cycle of living paycheck to paycheck, so you can start building your financial future. A life of financial freedom is absolutely possible, and the simple steps and strategies in this book will set you on your way to freedom.

Todd Tresidder
https://financialmentor.com

HOW TO BREAK THROUGH THE CONSTRAINTS THAT LIMIT YOUR SUCCESS

GIVE ME A LEVER LONG ENOUGH AND A PLACE TO STAND
AND I WILL MOVE THE ENTIRE EARTH.

– ARCHIMEDES

It seemed impossible to achieve. I had backed myself into a corner with my old business model, and there was no way to move forward.

FinancialMentor.com was already a lucrative financial coaching business, but the revenue model was maxed out because I couldn't work more hours. There was just *one of me* to coach the clients and only so many hours in a day. Worse yet, the prospective clients only wanted to work with *me* and would not accept a referral to other coaches. I had hit a wall.

I wanted to transition the business from a coaching services revenue model to a product-based business model. My goal was to build out a series of educational courses and books that "put Todd in a box" so that my knowledge gained over three decades in the financial business could reach more people at a more affordable price point – but how could I get it done?

I wasn't willing to work more hours, and I lacked the skills to build the new business model that was required. Special technology skills were necessary to build out the course platform, configure the sales process, and connect all the online automation systems so they communicated properly. I didn't know how to do any of that.

Also, new skills were required to write, edit, and market the books and courses, but I had no experience in that field either. As for the website, it needed a redesign to reorient the user experience so that it converted to educational products. I didn't know how to do any of that, and I didn't have the time to get any of it done.

However, once I defined all these constraints (and more!) that were preventing me from achieving my goals, the answer became obvious – leverage.

I employed *time leverage* by hiring a new assistant to manage social media, site administration, and the content post-production tasks like image creation, video production, and editing. I employed *experience leverage* in the form of a technology consultant, who then employed *systems leverage* through third-party software packages to connect all the online business systems that ran the course, the mailing lists, and the sales conversion processes to ensure they worked together. I didn't know how to do any of that myself. I never have.

I brought in a user experience expert to redesign the website so it featured the courses and books, and I even leveraged my personal wealth back into the business to pay the bills while the income lagged during the transition from service to product revenue.

In short, I achieved what was impossible to accomplish *alone* by overcoming every obstacle to my goals through multiple types of leverage – time, experience, systems, communications, marketing, and financial leverage.

Every obstacle that stood between me and my goals was solved with leverage; and every constraint that limited growth was overcome with leverage.

Now there's an entire team of experts behind me that implement technology, programming, business systems, sales systems, admin systems, SEO, editing, product development, copywriting, and much more. In fact, I'm employing every form of leverage that you'll learn about in this book, and *you* could do the same.

My financial education business wouldn't exist without leverage, and my wealth wouldn't exist without leverage.

Leverage is how I get more done with less of my own resources, and *you* can learn to do the same.

THE REAL REASON YOU'RE NOT AS RICH AS YOU SHOULD BE...

I share the example of my business to demonstrate a critically important point about leverage illustrated by the following question:

What is limiting your financial growth and profits so you're not making as much as you could right now?

- Not enough customers?
- A lousy boss?
- Not enough time?
- Not enough knowledge?
- Need another degree or credential?

Ask 20 people this question, and you'll get 20 different answers, but what's interesting is that nearly all the answers look in the wrong direction. They focus on *maximizing potential income*, but the real problem is *eliminating obstacles*.

In other words, your fastest path to forward momentum is to identify the constraints to your success and *remove* them. This is a key principle.

In the online business example, my constraints to growth included all aspects of content marketing and product development. I could develop the greatest products in the world, but I would still fail without targeted traffic generated through content marketing, or without the technology to scale the business through systems.

Conversely, I could develop amazing content marketing, driving hungry hordes of targeted traffic, but lack of any products to sell would be the limiting constraint in the business.

The point is that every business and personal wealth plan is limited by unique constraints, or bottlenecks, to growth. Your fastest path to improved results is to *identify those constraints and use leverage to overcome them.*

Changing the example to real estate, imagine that you ran across an amazing deal on an apartment building through a friend of a friend, and it's only because of this personal connection (network leverage) that you have first crack at it. The only problem is that you have no money for the down payment (constraint) and you have credit problems (constraint).

In that situation, most people would assume that they couldn't buy the building, so they'd miss out on the deal. *But after reading this book, you'll know how to leverage other people's money and credit to overcome whatever constraints you face so you can harvest that kind of opportunity.*

The point is to develop a two-pronged attack when pursuing success. You still want to set goals and move forward to maximize your potential, as is commonly taught in success literature, but it's actually *more* important to turn the analysis upside down and focus your attention not on where you want to go, but on *what holds you back* from getting there.

The key is to identify whatever aspect of the business is the *weakest*. If you have a great product but need marketing, then leverage solutions to overcome that constraint. Conversely, if you have great marketing but lack product to monetize with, then leverage your way to that solution. Whatever aspect of the business is the constraint to growth can be solved through *leverage*.

This distinction is critically important because it completely changes what actions you'll take and the results you'll produce. Your *constraints* identify your key leverage points for accelerating your wealth growth. Stated another way, leverage is the quickest, most direct path to overcoming your constraints.

For example, let's assume one of your financial goals is to buy five positive cash flow 4-plex apartment buildings over the next two years. The typical approach would be to learn about real estate investing so you can figure out how to accomplish your goal. That's the forward-looking process, and there's nothing wrong with that approach except that it's not the most efficient way to produce results.

The reason is that as you continue, you'll come face-to-face with your key constraints – you need the cash for the down-payments, and you need quality deal flow. It doesn't matter how much you drive your plan forward, because without those two resources you won't achieve your goal. They are the *key constraints* to your plan, and not coincidentally, the solution is *leverage*. You can leverage other people's money for the down-payments and other people's networks to access deal flow.

The point is that constraints are your quickest path to improving results, and the way you overcome your constraints is through leverage.

YOU DON'T NEED TO BE SMART, OR CREATIVE, OR HAVE A BIG NETWORK TO DO THIS

Let's look at another example to make this leverage strategy clear.

Success in business requires that you have some, if not all, of these characteristics:

- Intelligence
- Expertise
- Talent
- Knowledge
- A strong network

Your success can also be impacted by how much money you have, your personality, your experience, and your creativity.

But what if none of these were actually required?

Each of the listed traits will *contribute* to your potential for success, but they absolutely, positively won't *determine* your success. There's a huge gap between potential for success and actual success.

The key idea is: if you're lacking in any of these valid contributors, it's a constraint that can hold you back. It's the same principle as in the previous example, except that you're now applying it to your *personal skillset* rather than the characteristics of your business.

The problem with personal constraints is: they force you to work harder than necessary to grow less than your potential. They act like boat anchors holding you down.

But the good news is that your constraint problems are all solvable because *leverage* is how you break free of your personal constraints. It's how you grow beyond your own limitations.

That point is so important that it merits repeating: *leverage is how you break free of the personal constraints that hold you back because it gives you access to all the resources and skills that you lack.* Think about this for a moment because it has enormous implications for your life and your wealth.

The fact is: you could be missing most of these personal characteristics that lead to success and still be wildly successful, because all of them can be put to work for your benefit using leverage. It's a tremendously freeing concept.

And best of all, leverage is not some arcane secret-of-the-rich, and there's nothing stopping you from using it right now (except, of course, yourself). It's straightforward once you understand how it works. Whatever you don't know or can't do, somebody else knows more or can do it better than you. Whatever resources you lack, somebody else has.

4 THINGS YOU THINK YOU KNOW THAT JUST AIN'T SO!

Imagine you've been struggling to get your new business off the ground, but good news is on the horizon. All your hard work is about to pay off because a large national media company is going to publish a glowing review of your product. All of that media exposure (marketing leverage) is sure to lead to a surge in sales.

That's when most business owners would get scared…

- How is my existing staff going to handle the onslaught of new orders?

- Can I train them in time?

- What happens if I incur all the training and employee expenses, but the orders don't materialize as planned? How much will I lose?

- How much product will I need?

- How will I pay for all that inventory before the expected sales?

While the opportunity excites you, as the business owner you're also scared. You'll have to make some big bets and incur some huge risks. A lot can go wrong, and every potential mistake could be expensive.

Fortunately, you're a master of leverage, so you've planned for this moment from the day you began building your business. You designed your company with scalability in mind, and you developed leveraged growth strategies that manage all those risks.

Because of your savvy planning, the manufacturing company that provides your product has plenty of additional capacity for you to leverage and has agreed to give you 90-day payment terms *(financial leverage)* during your expansion phase – because they stand to benefit from your growth as well. In addition, you completely automated your order processing *(systems leverage)* to prepare for this moment, so it will fully scale at volume with no increase in cost; and you sub-contracted *(leveraged)* all product fulfillment to a large fulfillment warehouse specializing in that service. They charge on a per-unit basis with declining unit costs as the volume of sales increases, and they have plenty of extra capacity to scale with the increased order flow. In addition, all communications for the entire product cycle, from manufacturing through order placement to fulfillment, and all the way through customer activation, are completely automated and systemized *(systems leverage)*, so they scale automatically without increased cost.

In short, you prepared for this moment from the day you began building your business by integrating smart leverage strategies (that control risk and increase profits) into every aspect of the business. So you don't have to risk the family farm to scale up for your big media appearance. Oprah Winfrey could call tomorrow, and you'd be ready for the volume, and if Oprah never calls, you'd still operate safely and efficiently. Heads you win; tails you win.

This is an example of how leverage can be used to make more while risking less. It's not fiction; it's power. But like all tools of power, some will use it wisely, others will abuse it, and still others will fear it.

That's because *leverage* is something of a loaded term that can cause an emotional response in people due to common misunderstandings about how it works. Here are some examples of misconceptions and myths about leverage:

1. Leverage should only be utilized by investors with the highest risk tolerance.

2. If you leverage a person's skill or time, you're *using* them.

3. Leverage strategies are difficult or expensive to implement.

4. The loss potential is infinite.

The only form of leverage that inherently increases risk is *financial leverage*. It's the only type of leverage that always cuts both ways, making the good times great and the bad times unbearable. Financial leverage is the one strategy you have to be very careful with.

All other forms of leverage – time, technology, marketing, network, or experience – can actually increase results while reducing risk at the same time. When used properly, they can give you the best of both worlds.

WALKING THE TALK

I'm not just theorizing about the idea of leverage. I built my career around this concept, and for two decades I've coached clients to do the same – *because it works.*

My career experience has spanned three distinct stages, each tightly correlated to leverage. I started my career as a hedge fund investment manager in paper assets, and then became a real estate investor in large apartment buildings and tax liens, and now I'm an infopreneur teaching through online courses and books.

- Why did I pick hedge fund investment management over the more obvious choice of becoming a traditional financial advisor? Probably 999 out of 1000 people pursuing a financial career straight out of college would have chosen the latter, but I chose the former.

- Why did I pick large apartment buildings and tax liens for my real estate investing rather than the much easier single family homes? Again, probably 999 out of 1000 people starting into real estate would have chosen the latter.

- And why did I pick online courses and books for my financial education business at https://financialmentor.com rather than giving seminars or teaching in a University setting?

The answer in every case boils down to one word – leverage. I've always chosen high-leverage business models over the low-leverage alternatives, even when the high-leverage choice was less common and much more difficult. Each choice was a conscious, pro-active decision to pursue more leverage, rather than less.

High-leverage business has the potential for far greater success. When you get it right, profits can grow geometrically because it's baked into the cake of the underlying characteristics of each business. Whereas low-leverage businesses are inherently limited by your personal resources, so they can never scale into something substantial.

The high potential payoff of the leveraged alternative justifies risking my time; whereas the low potential payoff of the unleveraged alternative isn't worth paying the price of my (or your) scarcest resource – time.

IN SUMMARY

Leverage is simply another tool that you're going to master so you can strategically employ it in your wealth plan in order to overcome the constraints that limit your growth. It's not inherently good or bad; it's just a tool that allows you to impact your world and develop your financial potential in a more effective manner.

Leverage doesn't inherently increase risk (unless it's financial leverage), but it does increase results, and that's why it's an essential tool for you to include in your wealth plan.

PRINCIPLES: THE 9 PRINCIPLES OF LEVERAGE

THE TOP 9 PRINCIPLES FOR MASTERING LEVERAGE IN RECORD TIME

THE SHORTEST AND SUREST WAY OF ARRIVING AT REAL
KNOWLEDGE IS TO UNLEARN THE LESSONS WE HAVE BEEN
TAUGHT, TO MOUNT THE FIRST PRINCIPLES, AND TAKE
NOBODY'S WORD ABOUT THEM.

—HENRY BOLINGBROKE

Now that you know what leverage is, and why nobody gets rich without it, the next step is to uncover the principles that determine how leverage works so you can put it to use in your wealth plan.

This chapter covers the first (and most difficult) of the nine principles of leverage that you need to understand before you can overcome the constraints that limit your life. Stick with me through this first foundational principle and the rest of the leverage principles will be easier to digest.

PRINCIPLE 1: MATHEMATICAL EXPECTANCY

Mathematical expectancy is how you convert an unknowable and uncertain future into statistical confidence. It's how you convert doubt into a predictable outcome.

When you understand how mathematical expectancy works, it will change how you play the wealth building game forever.

IT'S ALL ABOUT EXPECTANCY

Expectancy and the closely related strategies of risk management and leverage are the three most important factors determining your financial success.

That's because all wealth is math, and there are two equations that govern how your wealth grows. The *mathematical expectancy equation* determines your compound growth rate, and the *future value equation* determines what it will grow to, and by what date. When you combine these two equations, you have a complete framework for understanding your wealth growth process.

Unfortunately, most people have only a vague understanding of how expectancy works or what it means. Most people are turned off by math so the topic is rarely discussed in the press or in bestselling business books.

But this is unfortunate. Readers are missing out because mathematical expectancy proves that wealth planning is a rational, duplicable science that can be reduced to equations and principles that are safe and smart to use. These equations define the scope and shape of the process by forming boundaries around the knowledge required, which then provides a clear direction for best practices.

More importantly, mathematical expectancy is particularly interesting because it converts the uncertainty of an unknowable future into a plannable process that is clear and scientific, and that has predictable outcomes.

HOW EXPECTANCY AND PROBABILITY INTERACT IN THE REAL WORLD

Expectancy goes by many names, including expectation, mathematical expectation, EV, average, mean value, mean, or first moment.

What it tells you is how much you can expect to make, on average, per dollar risked. That definition clearly connects expectancy to your wealth growth, so let's look at the formula:

$$\text{EXPECTED VALUE} = (\text{PROBABILITY OF WIN} * \text{AVERAGE WIN}) - (\text{PROBABILITY OF LOSS} * \text{AVERAGE LOSS})$$

While that's pretty straightforward, let's make it even simpler and more intuitive by reducing it to just two variables: probability times payoff. It's the probability of something occurring multiplied by the payoff when it occurs.

In other words, you already understand probability, which is the odds of something occurring. Everybody gets that. A fair coin has 50% odds of heads coming up on any flip. Expectancy simply adds one more dimension by multiplying the probability of something occurring times the payoff you get when it occurs.

For example, what happens if heads pays $5 and tails loses $2? And how does expectancy change when heads pays $7, but tails loses $8? Those questions are answered by expectancy, not probability. So what you should notice is how *probability* is the odds of something occurring, but *expectancy* tells you the financial impact those occurrences have, and that's where *leverage* comes into play.

The key thing to notice is how the payoff dimension completely changes the math. It converts the already intuitive odds of something occurring into something different – something that eludes most people because you're not trained to think in terms of two dimensions with a payoff variable.

Expectancy is the result of how much you make when you're right, minus how much you lose when you're wrong, multiplied by how frequently you're right or wrong. That net number is the average amount you expect to make each time you put your capital at risk, which determines your return on investment in your future value equation.

HOW TO CONVERT UNCERTAINTY INTO OPPORTUNITY!

Now that you know expectancy determines the growth of your wealth, let's switch gears and connect all the logic blocks I've shared so far into a single picture that shows you how it all fits together and ties leverage into your wealth planning strategy.

- **Expectancy analysis is how you estimate outcomes that are uncertain.** The fact that all your investments and business plans to build wealth are a bet on an unknowable future is, by definition, an uncertain outcome. That's why expectancy analysis is required. It's the scientific, reliable way to manage the risk of the unknown.

- **Expectancy analysis is how you make smart financial decisions when all outcomes are uncertain.** It gives you a scientific, rational way to reduce risk and maximize reward using leverage that converts unknowable outcomes into the closest thing to certainty you can get (without a crystal ball).

- **The formula is really nothing more than probability times payoff.** This stuff isn't complicated, but it's counterintuitive because we all think in terms of the odds of something occurring. Introducing payoff to the equation literally changes how you play the wealth building game. Yes, it's that important. It becomes a two-part, dynamic equation where unlikely events with very large payoffs, either negative or positive, have a disproportionately outsized influence on results.

- **Disproportionate results have make-or-break impacts on the compound return equation.** The key principle of risk management is to control your plans so you can control outsized negative payoffs, commonly known as losses, from destroying your expectancy, and consequently your wealth growth. Leverage is how you maximize the gains from your winning decisions.

- **Designing your wealth plan to maximize gains through leverage while minimizing losses through risk management is how you tilt the payoff portion of the expectancy equation.** If you can favorably tilt the payoff portion of the equation enough, then you can still profit even if you lose more often than you win. That's how you create reliable profits out of unreliable, unpredictable future outcomes.

- **Seek large, positive investment returns using leverage so you can win big when you succeed; but learn how to control risk for adverse losses during the inevitable failures by using risk management strategies.** (This is taught in a separate book in this series, *Risk Management – How To Make More By Losing Less*, and it's also taught in the risk management mini-course found at https://financialmentor.com/educational-products/risk-management-course.) When you shoot for large positive outcomes when you're right, while controlling risk to small negative outcomes when you're wrong, you effectively tilt the expectancy equation to result in *wealth*. It's literally as simple as that; but of course, the devil is in the details, which is what we'll get to in the remaining chapters of this book. But your overriding goal for leverage is to *tilt* the payoff dimension of the expectancy equation, which is the dimension you have the most control over.

• **Understanding all the implications of expectancy, and mastering the required skills of leverage and risk management as implied by expectancy analysis, are central to your financial success.** It's the single best way to take back control of your financial life from all the uncertainty inherent in putting capital at risk in an unknowable future.

I'm sure that's a mouthful if you're not familiar with these ideas, but I wanted to give you a step-by-step flow of how the logic connects – from uncertainty about an unknowable future to risk management and leverage strategies that control losses and maximize gains, thus tilting the payoff part of the equation to result in positive expectancy, or wealth growth. Again, here's the equation:

$$\text{EXPECTED VALUE} =$$
$$\text{(PROBABILITY OF WIN} * \text{AVERAGE WIN)} -$$
$$\text{(PROBABILITY OF LOSS} * \text{AVERAGE LOSS)}$$

MANAGE YOUR PAYOFF TO MASTER YOUR WEALTH GROWTH

The counterintuitive realization is that disproportionate payoffs can make you rich if you maximize gains through leverage when you're right and manage the risk tightly when you're wrong. *Even if you're wrong 9 times out of 10, or even 99 times out of 100, you can still profit by tilting the payoff portion of the equation.* My suggestion is that you *highlight that sentence in gold* because it explains how you can reliably achieve your financial goals when facing an uncertain future.

Equally as important, you'll want to realize how a strategy that produces mostly winning investments can still be a loser with negative expectancy if the average loss is *larger* than the average win. In fact, many investing strategies are notorious for that problem.

THE TRAP OF NEEDING TO WIN

But focusing on *payoff* is counterintuitive to most people because it's not how we're trained to think. I believe it's a major reason that wealth eludes most people. We all have a natural bias toward winning with high *reliability*.

You *want* to be right. It feels good to win, and nobody likes to lose. We're taught in school that high accuracy gets an A, and mediocre accuracy equals failure. Nothing below 70% correct is even acceptable, which is absurd. Even worse, many people mistakenly view failure as a measure of self-worth.

Everyone is looking for high reliability because we're trained to think in terms of probability, but the percentage of winners versus losers is not the most important factor to your financial success, and it's the thing you have the least control over. The real key to expectancy is *how you control losses and maximize gains – through risk management and leverage.*

It's irrational to focus on winning versus losing because, as I said earlier, the future is uncertain, so it's not really within your control. You should always try your best to win, but the reality is: if you play the game, losses are inevitable. It's just a fact of life when the future is unknowable.

For example, I lose all the time. It's a regular part of every week of my life. I never really get used to it because I'm human like everyone else, but I've trained myself to accept that putting capital at risk into an unknowable future means that losing is an inevitable part of the investment process and I have to accept that.

But *payoffs* are different. I actively manage my payoffs because that's the part of the equation that's controllable; and fortunately, the math is clear: if you do a good job of controlling losses, you can get rich relatively easily. It's just a question of sample size.

The bottom line is: successful wealth builders are fine with losing more often than they'd like, but they're very attached to the relative size of those wins and losses because that's what's really important to your financial outcome in life.

Think of risk management as the *defensive* half of your wealth plan to tilt payoff in the expectancy equation; and think of leverage as the *offensive* half of your wealth plan to tilt payoff. They each tilt payoff favorably, but in opposite directions.

When you put both leverage and risk management together in your wealth plan, the net effect is to radically tilt your payoff to such an extreme degree that your success becomes a matter of sample size. It's not a question of *if;* it's a question of *when.* All you have to do is implement both disciplines with persistence.

IN SUMMARY

Mathematical Expectancy can be somewhat counterintuitive because most people are conditioned to think in terms of *probability*, not expectancy. Expectancy is *probability times payoff*, and adding that payoff component to the equation changes everything.

Your wealth compounds according to *expectancy*, not probability. Introducing the payoff component to the equation emphasizes the essential role that risk management and leverage both play in your wealth growth. Risk management minimizes losses, and leverage maximizes gains. Together, they can create positive expectancy and wealth growth even if you lose far more often than you win (low probability of success).

Payoff is particularly important because the future is unknowable, so controlling probability is difficult. You can guesstimate probability, but it's ultimately unknowable. However, you *can* control payoff.

Smart wealth builders focus on those things they can control so they can produce a predictably profitable outcome regardless of circumstances. Mathematical expectancy gives you the framework to achieve that objective, and leverage is the tool you use to create large wins, thus tilting the payoff equation and creating positive mathematical expectancy.

EXERCISE: EXPECTANCY ANALYSIS

Imagine you've accumulated a $50,000 "war chest" and set it aside to launch your dream business. You're presented with quite a few business "opportunities" to consider. They all look promising, or you wouldn't be considering them, but the future is always unknown so every one of them could fail.

Your task in this exercise is to flex your expectancy analysis muscles so you can get in the practice of maximizing your expectancy with every decision. Analyze each deal both in terms of probability of success and in terms of potential payoff versus loss. Also, notice the overall risk to your entire nest egg from *a single deal* versus situations where risk can be controlled so you can try *multiple deals* in a series should any one deal fail.

- The first business is a local sandwich shop. You can buy it from the current owner for $25K, and this includes all equipment and inventory. The owner's records show it earns $100K per year after paying employees, but that doesn't include paying the owner. The owner's sole revenue is the profit from the shop. Additionally, nearly all of the profit comes from lunch rush hour during the business week when there is a line-up out the door and the shop is producing all the sandwiches it's capable of producing. At other times the shop has limited business.

- The second opportunity is your dream coaching business. Good coaches make $150 to $250 per hour, with top coaches fetching higher rates. The problem is that most coaches starve for lack of clients because they have no marketing system. To figure your real income potential, you have to include all the costs, both time and money, for marketing your practice when no revenue is produced. The good news is you have $50K to survive on until you get it working – if you work at it full time. Assuming you figure out, in that limited time, a marketing model that converts clients, remember that your coaching income is limited by the hours you can work, given that the revenue model is trading time for money.

- The third opportunity is an innovative new product created by your gadget buddy. He just came up with an idea that seems like a break-through, and you've guesstimated that it will cost $50K to take it from idea to fully proven prototype ready for manufacturing. (What a coincidence! It's the exact amount of money you've saved). You've already identified the ideal target market for this product and you've run the idea past five people in that market with all of them asking: "Where can I buy it?" The profit margin on the product would be large, but there are a lot of unknowns since you're starting from scratch with no proven business model.

- The fourth opportunity is an options trading course claiming that you can make a full time living by trading options. After buying the course, you'd still have enough money left over to fund your options trading business (according to the salesperson). You've asked for referrals, and they all seem like good people, but none of them are making a fulltime living yet. In addition, you were researching the basic premise of the course and you came across a very negative article on the subject, built around the idea of infrequent, but regularly occurring, "fat-tail risk" issues with these strategies. The course salesman says they've got it handled, but the article implies there's more to understand and the references you were given don't seem to have any clue about these issues.

Analyze each opportunity above by answering the following questions:

- What exactly are you risking? Time, money, other resources?

- How much are you risking? Can the risk be carefully controlled?

- If it fails, will you have enough resources to get up to bat again, or will it take you out of the game?

- How would you measure "failure"? Is it losing money; is it failing to meet your goals in life; or what?

- What's the probability for success? (Be practical. You're not looking for an exact number, but you can at least tell which choices are high probability versus low probability.)

- How do you measure "success"? If financial success, is it the degree of fulfillment, or what?

- Could the opportunity ever result in a life-changing "big" win that tilts the payoff equation, or is it inherently limited?

- Could the opportunity ever result in a life-changing loss that tilts the payoff equation negatively, or is it controllable?

Success for this exercise is not coming up with the "right" answer, because (just like in life) there is no right answer that's knowable from analysis alone. Only in the fullness of time is the "right" answer known with 20/20 hindsight.

Success for this exercise is to train your mind to habitually think in terms of *expectancy*, and to begin viewing all life decisions through *mathematical* expectancy – because it has life-changing consequences. And if this challenges you to complete on your own then download the companion bonus package you get with this book. It includes a free audio recording where I analyze each business with a group of fellow students. You can download the entire bonus package for free at https://financialmentor.com/free-stuff/leverage-book.

For example, expectancy analysis can change your eating habits, exercise habits, prioritization of relationships, work projects, occupation, and much, much more. Yes, it's that big of a deal. The outcome of your life will be determined by mathematical expectancy at many levels. You can either develop the habitual thinking pattern that makes it work in your favor, or you can endure the negative payoff.

THE PRINCIPLES TO LEVERAGE LIMITED RESOURCES

WHEN A MAN TELLS YOU THAT HE GOT RICH
THROUGH HARD WORK, ASK HIM: "WHOSE?"

– DON MARQUIS

Now that you've got the math fundamentals out of the way, it's time to dive into a few principles that will be intuitive. These are the ones that are easier to see and feel the truth of. This chapter is going to explain how leverage can overcome limited resources to create exponential growth.

PRINCIPLE 2: TRADING TIME FOR MONEY LIMITS WEALTH GROWTH

What's the most valuable non-renewable resource you have?

Obviously, it's your time.

You aren't making more. You can't buy more. When it's spent, it's gone.

And if you're trading that ultra-limited resource for

money, you're limiting your economic life to reciprocal forms of exchange, which is the hidden problem in most wealth plans.

But it's not just trading time for money. Reciprocal exchange also includes trading your money for a product or a fixed interest rate of return. It means you exchange one thing of value for something of equal value.

There's nothing wrong with reciprocal exchange when you have average goals, but it limits your ability to achieve financial independence.

For example, wage-earning W-2 employment can provide a nice income and lifestyle, but unless there is scalable upside potential through equity options or income growth participation, there is no leverage, which limits your ability to create a big win that tilts the payoff portion of your expectancy equation.

The problem with reciprocal income is that you're limited to your personal resources because that's all you have to exchange. Unfortunately, you can only work so many hours per day for so many weeks per year before you run out of years, and somewhere in between you're supposed to enjoy your life.

Similarly, conventional asset allocation in paper assets (stocks, bonds, and mutual funds) is governed by strict mathematical limits to growth that is unfortunately beyond the scope of this book to explain (but is fully explained in both my Expectancy Wealth Planning course and my Expectancy Investing courses). For the purposes of this book, one of the drivers behind that limited growth is the lack of leverage involved. Sure, there's some leverage in stock ownership, since you own a share of the company that, over time, will hopefully grow due to inflation and employee skill; but bonds offer no real leverage because they're a form of reciprocal payment where you exchange value for value (in this case, you lend a fixed amount of capital for a fixed amount of interest).

Notice how these reciprocal exchanges of time and money – your two primary resources – are not benefiting from leverage? That's the problem with traditional wealth plans that lack leverage. They're based primarily on reciprocal exchange.

That's why the traditional plan typically takes a lifetime to achieve financial independence (with the sole exception of extreme frugality); but a *leveraged* plan can work much faster, without resorting to extreme frugality, by applying principles that increase the mathematical expectancy.

PRINCIPLE 3: THE OPPORTUNITY COST PROBLEM

The core problem with reciprocal exchange is that your resources of time and money are limited.

Time and money spent in one place cannot be used elsewhere. There's an opportunity cost to choosing to spend it in one way and not in another. At some point, your financial growth hits a wall.

The way it works is: you trade a unit of time for a unit of money, and then you add those units together to get a paycheck. Then you exchange this paycheck for the limited version of goods and services you can afford from the unlimited supply that you have to pick from. The more you make, the more you spend, and your savings gets what's left over (if anything) after taxes and lifestyle spending take their cut.

When you limit yourself to your own resources, you're without leverage. You have to rely on your own time, contacts, experience, money, and other resources. That's why the three most expensive words in the English language are: "Do it yourself." Relying on yourself only *hinders* your success.

Leverage gives you access to time and resources other than your own so you can produce greater results faster *using less of your own time and money.*

PRINCIPLE 4: TIME FREEDOM

Quick exercise: jot down what percentage of your day is spent trading time for money.

Now, how much of your day is spent creating leveraged growth?

If you want to know how long it will take you to become financially independent, just look at how much of your day is spent trading time for money versus how much of your day is spent creating leveraged growth. The greater the proportion of time dedicated to leveraged growth, the faster the path to your goal.

You can apply that rule to both of your primary resources – time and money – but *time* is really the driving force.

For example, just imagine if you were never going to die, thus giving you unlimited time. You wouldn't need leverage because you could eventually satiate your desire for anything in the world. The smallest savings rate would eventually compound to a magnificent fortune, given unlimited time. That fortune could buy anything you desired, and any goal that mattered to you could be achieved, given incremental progress over an unlimited amount of time.

The fact that time is limited is what sets the deadline (literally!) that makes the financial acceleration through leverage so incredibly important to the quality of your life.

- Think of leverage as the science of creating sources of income that aren't dependent on your time.

- Successfully applying leverage releases you from certain time limitations so you can pursue fulfillment.

- Leverage is the tool you use to buy back your life by achieving financial freedom faster, so less of your life is spent on money pursuits.

The successful application of leverage gives you the freedom to do what's important to you in life and what aligns with your deepest values... without worrying about money.

IN SUMMARY

The reason leverage is so important is because your personal resources (time and money) are limited. If you had unlimited time and money, leverage would be unnecessary because the purpose of leverage is to overcome those inherent limitations we all face.

Most people limit their financial growth by engaging in a reciprocal exchange of their limited resources. They trade their time for money, or they trade their money for a limited return.

Eventually, you run into opportunity cost limitations where you can't trade any more time to produce any more money because you're already working as much as you can tolerate. There has to be a better way....

Leverage is how you overcome all of your personal limitations, including your primary resource limitations of time and money. Leverage gives you access to more time and money than you personally possess, so you can produce greater results faster using less of your own time and money.

EXERCISE: TIME TRACKING 1

This is a fun and revealing exercise.

One of my favorite ideas is that if you want to know how long it will take you to become financially independent, just look at how much of your day is spent trading time for money (or just pissing money away) versus how much of your day is spent creating leveraged growth.

Mark a calendar into 30-minute increments and track it for two weeks. Label each 30-minute increment as dedicated to leveraged growth, or not.

This practice is eye-opening because it will literally reveal if you are fast-tracking or slow-tracking your wealth plans.

Worksheets for this exercise (and all exercises for this book) can be downloaded absolutely free at https://financialmentor.com/free-stuff/leverage-book).

Are you spending the bulk of your time dedicated to leveraged growth strategies, or are you doing other things? The answer to this question will be a major determinant of your financial outcome in life.

GROW WEALTHY BY PROVIDING VALUE AND SOLVING PROBLEMS

ALL LIFE IS PROBLEM SOLVING.

— KARL POPPER

What if I told you that leverage can even help you take care of your kids for date night? I'll explain that in a minute. The point is: it's not always about making money.

Sure, financial independence is an incredibly valuable goal, but some people remain uncomfortable pursuing leverage because they feel like they're using people or asking for a favor.

We've all been "used" by someone before, and it's a lousy feeling. Nobody wants that. Which is why leverage done right is the opposite because it's about helping and giving to others.

You know you're helping and giving to others when you can answer "yes" to the following two questions:

- Are you giving more value than you're taking?
- Are you solving a problem for the person being leveraged?

If you answered "no" to either of these questions, then you're likely more focused on what you want than what the other person wants. Your plans will be experienced by others as manipulative.

To understand how this works, you must shift your thinking from the reciprocal exchange model, where you trade *time* for dollars, to trading *value* for dollars – because value can be provided in many different ways.

PRINCIPLE 5: GROW WEALTHY BY PROVIDING VALUE AND SOLVING PROBLEMS

Your goal is to figure out how to give more value and solve more problems by asking the following two questions:

- How can I give more of my unique skills and talents to benefit more people?

- What are all the different ways I can give more value so that my plans are clearly in the other person's best interests?

The common thread to all of these questions is "giving more." That's how you benefit everyone you do business with so nobody feels used.

Think of it from the other side of the table. The only reason someone welcomes your plans to leverage their time and resources is because it *benefits* them. People do what is in their best interests, so your goal is to design leveraged wealth plans that provide greater value and solve problems for all involved.

For example, I negotiated the purchase of a 102-unit apartment building using none of my own money. The purchase price was significantly below market value. In addition, the loan package I assembled was difficult to negotiate but added value to the property and cash flow for the new buyers.

In exchange for negotiating the purchase and loan, I received 10% of the property, or 10.2 apartment units, without using any of my own money. I didn't even have to run the deal after the close. All I had to do was organize it and close it, and in return, I received ten apartment units for zero out of pocket and zero additional obligations.

The seller was happy because I solved a problem for him. The building had issues that made it complicated to negotiate and close. He was old and sick and needed it out of his estate for personal planning reasons; and he was extremely wealthy, so the price wasn't his primary concern. It had already fallen out of escrow three times, so he sold it to me at a severe discount because he believed I had the skill to close the deal and solve a problem for him.

The investors were elated because I gave them more value than I took. They got access to a property that they couldn't have bought without my skills and that doubled their money at the closing table.

I leveraged the investors' money and solved the seller's problem, and both the seller and the buyers leveraged my network, real estate knowledge, negotiation skills, and business skills. Everyone involved in the transaction benefited.

At this point you might be thinking: "This leverage stuff is easy for you, Todd, because you have all that financial knowledge." But these principles are universally applicable and aren't just limited to finance and real estate.

My wife and her friends leverage each other for affordable and trustworthy childcare. When my kids were small, the various moms took turns watching each other's children while the other mom ran errands, exercised, or just caught her breath for a while. The kids happily entertained each other on these play dates, so the women got more done while spending less effort and money and they got better childcare as well – plus it was great socialization for the kids. Everyone benefited.

This network of moms also leveraged each other's contacts. If one mom knew of a good babysitter, and the other was in a bind for date-night, the network would come to the rescue. If another mom had a great experience with a house painter or handyman, suddenly that guy got booked solid as his name worked through the network. Again, everyone benefited.

That's the beauty of leverage properly applied: it not only builds wealth for you; it also helps and gives to others in the process, so everyone is better off. As you develop these skills, you'll achieve greater success with less effort, and you'll help your friends in the process.

IN SUMMARY

One of the keys to mastering leverage is to break free of reciprocal exchange limitations resulting from the false belief that all you have to give is time or money. What people really want is *value*, and they will gladly give you their time or money if you can deliver enough value. In addition, there are an unlimited number of ways to give value.

The key to giving value in every transaction is to make sure you're giving more than you're taking, or to make sure you're solving a problem for the person that's worth more than the price they pay for the solution.

Your goal is to give *more* – more of your talents, skills, experience, insights, network, resources, and anything else you can share. It's a tremendously satisfying way to build your wealth because your financial growth becomes a measure of how much you've given to others.

EXERCISE: IDENTIFY POTENTIAL LEVERAGE POINTS

The purpose of this exercise is for you to identify your high-value skills and knowledge that should be leveraged.

The example I gave showing my high-value leverage

points included my financial knowledge and my coaching experience. It's an unusual combination of skill and knowledge that can deliver great value to people and should be leveraged to help more people solve more problems.

What are your high-value leverage skills and interests that can result in you massively growing income and wealth as you succeed? Commit them to writing.

The point is to think in terms of developing a big-win game plan. Don't settle for mediocrity. Think in terms of how you can scale your knowledge and skills to deliver more value and solve more problems for more people.

MAKE YOURSELF UNNECESSARY

I'D RATHER HAVE 1% OF THE EFFORT OF 100 MEN
THAN 100% OF MY OWN EFFORT.

– J. PAUL GETTY

You can't leverage every aspect of your life. There are limits to this tool.

For example, you still have to do your own pushups if you want to get in shape. The only person who can play the husband role with my wife is me (or we're both in trouble). Only I can be a daddy to my children. Only I can take care of my health, write my books and courses, and interview for media appearances. I can't leverage any of these activities.

But the number of roles and tasks in your life that can be leveraged greatly exceeds the limited number of roles that can't. Deciding which roles to isolate and leverage depends on your interests, and on the skills and resources you bring to the table. You must identify your strengths and your weaknesses to know what work is best completed by you and what should be delegated.

For example, I have leveraged my financial knowledge over and over again in each business throughout my lifetime. That was unique to me, but yours will likely be different.

PRINCIPLE 6: MAKE YOURSELF UNNECESSARY

The principle you'll apply is to identify which high leverage activities make sense based on your skills and interests. You do this by identifying what things *you*, and *only you*, must do. Then you have someone else do the rest – because you'll achieve more, better, faster results through delegation and partnering. It also frees up your time and energy to focus on your strengths and gifts.

For example, I'm the only one with the expertise to write this book and create my courses. But other people can edit, produce, and market those products. Other people can do accounting, answer certain emails, and do any other task that isn't absolutely essential for me to complete.

One of the great entrepreneurial mistakes is falling prey to what Chris Ducker called the "Super-Hero Syndrome." It's a self-limiting belief built around the cultural notion of self-reliance that you can do it yourself better, or easier, or cheaper. You can't!

If your goals are wealth and freedom, the only way you can have both together is with the help of others. If you think you can't afford to get various types of assistance to accelerate your results, then you probably can't afford not to, and the real holdback is simply not knowing how to do it right.

You have to decide what your highest and best value is to the implementation of your wealth plan and then *delegate* the rest. If you can't deliver more value than what an employee in your organization costs then you don't deserve more than a normal wage because you have nothing worth leveraging. Harsh words, but it's also the honest truth.

You must identify the unique knowledge, systems, and abilities you can deliver that should be leveraged through employees and business systems to maximize the value you deliver to the world.

You can't know everything. My general rule is that if specialized technical knowledge is required, then it should probably be delegated. For example, all of my website programming and development at FinancialMentor.com is delegated to an expert who does nothing but focus on that skill all day, every day. Similarly, you shouldn't write your own legal contracts or perform your own brain surgery. Professionals specializing in these skills will always know more about their field of expertise than you could ever learn.

The point is you should only do what is absolutely necessary for you to do – where you are the required expert with the necessary skill. You'll never be the best at everything, so let other people shine by demonstrating their expertise. Make yourself unnecessary everywhere possible so you can focus your *limited* time on those few areas where you're truly necessary.

IN SUMMARY

Don't be a super-hero and try to do everything yourself. It's a fool's game because when you're the cog, then you're the clog. There's always more to be done than any one person can do. The more you try to do by yourself, the more you'll just slow your progress and place a ceiling on how successful you can become.

The smart strategy is to identify those tasks that only *you* can complete, and delegate the rest. Focus your limited time on the few activities where you're absolutely essential. Let others shine by doing everything else, thus leveraging other people's time to accomplish more while focusing your limited time on just the highest value activities requiring your attention.

EXERCISE: TIME TRACKING 2

Download the time tracking spreadsheet that is part of your free exercise workbook found at https://financial-mentor.com/free-stuff/leverage-book.

The purpose of this exercise is to identify and categorize *how* you spend your time, so you can pinpoint specific tasks that are either low value and should be delegated, or could be better performed by someone else with specialized skills.

The idea is: you should only do what produces the highest and best value for your time and what matches your special skill set.

Most people track their time using either an app on their smartphone or writing everything on a sheet of paper. The key is to tabulate all activities down to 30-minute intervals for *at least two weeks*.

1. Which activities are low value?

2. Which activities are high value?

3. Which activities can you potentially delegate?

4. What systems could replace certain activities?

5. Can you identify activities where *other people* might bring more skill and experience to the work than you?

6. Can you identify the activities where you, and *only you*, have the experience and skill required to complete the task and where nobody could be trained to replace you?

7. Which activities are constraints limiting your success – things that would accelerate your financial results if they were leveraged?

You will probably be able to identify many activities that consume your precious time but provide little financial return. Some may be necessary, but you may be able to eliminate others. Also, look for tasks that don't take *full* advantage of your talents. These tasks can usually be organized into standard operating procedures (SOP's) and delegated to someone whose skills perfectly match the task.

The way you do this is by examining items 1, 3, 4, 5 and 7 above as *potential delegation targets*. These are the obvious activities to get off your plate.

Next, figure out how you can allocate more productive time to work on items 2 and 6. How can you design your wealth plan so those activities are your focus going forward?

UPFRONT COSTS, BENEFITS LAG

"DELAYING GRATIFICATION IS A PROCESS OF
SCHEDULING THE PAIN AND PLEASURE OF LIFE IN SUCH
A WAY AS TO ENHANCE THE PLEASURE BY MEETING AND
EXPERIENCING THE PAIN FIRST AND GETTING IT OVER WITH.
IT'S THE ONLY DECENT WAY TO LIVE."

M. SCOTT PECK

Imagine the acceleration and growth in your wealth plan when you have an entire team of talented people with specialized skills that are perfectly matched with the responsibilities they've been delegated – far more skill than you could ever accumulate in several lifetimes – and all working toward a common goal. That is how great success is achieved.

But leverage like that costs money, and that's one of the biggest challenges you'll face. There is always an upfront cost that must be paid in terms of time, training, or system development before you can benefit from the results produced. And, of course, there is never a convenient time to incur those upfront costs.

Employees and contractors are expensive. Software and business systems have upfront capital and training costs before they produce results. Your natural inclination when cash flow is tight is to conserve capital by *doing it yourself*, but this may be the exact opposite of what you should do.

Using Financial Mentor as an example, my investment and coaching experience is unique and valuable. Rather than deliver it one-on-one to individual coaching clients, it makes good business sense to leverage that knowledge in the form of products, with the help of business systems and employees to provide the production, delivery, and support. The highest and best value I can deliver is to get that knowledge out of my head and organized into a product format so I can deliver more value to more people at a lower price point.

That all sounds good in theory, but it's really hard to do in practice because of the upfront cost and lagged results.

PRINCIPLE 7: UPFRONT COSTS, BENEFITS LAG

Consider the two scenarios: I could have a nice six-figure coaching practice working part-time, or I could spend years working full-time for nothing while I develop the educational curriculum, pay for employee support, pay for all the systems development that delivers Financial Mentor's products, and produce the marketing systems to sell the product – all before a single dime is made.

The issue is *lag*. When I trade time for money as a coach, there is no lag. But with leverage, you pay upfront long before the benefit shows up down the road. That lag frequently leads to the incorrect conclusion that you can't afford to delegate, when the truth is that you can't afford *not* to delegate. Lag is just a required part of the process that you have to endure.

I call it "bridging." You have to bridge the lag by trading time for money as you hustle to build leveraged sources of income that can scale. It takes time, and you have to remain solvent during that bridge time.

But there really is no other choice because without delegation, the alternative is that life will just get harder and harder – because the more successful you become, the harder you must work. In my case, I was taking on too many coaching clients as the demand rose and I was burning out.

However, with leverage, life gets easier the more successful you become – because you'll do less and less of the work as you increase your leverage, until you're only doing what is specifically required of you based on your unique skills and abilities.

Staying with this same example, I produce my books and courses *once* and I pay all costs upfront; but then I can sell them over and over, using systems leverage to deliver the value. It sounds good, but always remember that you must be willing to pay the price upfront in order to enjoy the benefits down the road – because of the principle of lag.

IN SUMMARY

Leverage seldom results in instant gratification. Instead, there's typically a price to pay upfront before you can enjoy the benefit later (otherwise known as lag). And there's never a convenient time to pay that price. Never.

If your goal is wealth and freedom, then you need to develop the habit of *delayed gratification*. You must embrace paying the price upfront and enduring the lag.

That requires you to bridge the lag. You must figure out how to pay your bills and get all the regular work done upfront before you see the benefits down the road. This usually means trading time for money temporarily while you build the leveraged sources of income that can scale.

EXERCISE: DELAY GRATIFICATION

Identify one wealth-building activity that involves delayed gratification, an activity that will benefit your life but that you're not currently implementing.

Maybe it's as simple as saving money. Or maybe it's as complex as creating new leveraged operating systems in your business that require specialized software expertise.

If you can't come up with an idea, then download *101 Leverage Hacks: A Cheat Sheet for Quickly Implementing Leverage in Your Wealth Plan*. It will give you lots of ideas to pick from (https://financialmentor.com/free-stuff/leverage-book).

Rinse and repeat, creating a list of all the different ways you could create leverage and grow wealth through delayed gratification. Focus on two categories of ideas:

- Easy to implement
- Scares you to think about implementing it.

Pick one idea from the "easy to implement" category and get it done now. Then pick another one so as to develop the habit of delayed gratification.

Next, look over your list of "scares you to implement" and choose the one idea that has the biggest potential payoff (remember the concept of 'expectancy' mathematics).

Develop a thorough risk management plan to implement that high-value strategy. Solve all the problems that stand between you and that big payoff.

Rinse and repeat until you develop the habit of delayed gratification.

EXPAND THE GAP

ANNUAL INCOME TWENTY POUNDS,
ANNUAL EXPENDITURE NINETEEN SIX, RESULT HAPPINESS.
ANNUAL INCOME TWENTY POUNDS, ANNUAL EXPENDITURE
TWENTY POUND OUGHT AND SIX, RESULT MISERY.

CHARLES DICKENS

The next leverage principle you'll want to apply in your wealth plan is expanding the gap between how much you earn and how much you spend, so it grows geometrically instead of arithmetically.

There's a natural progression to widening this gap. Most people start out as an employee – the producer in a reciprocal arrangement of time for money. The next stage in business development is usually self-employment, where you essentially buy yourself a job by doing most of the production. Unfortunately, this business model also lacks leverage.

PRINCIPLE 8: EXPAND THE GAP

The leveraged business owner removes himself from the production equation, so the business runs itself in his absence. You achieve this goal by converting everything you do into a step-by-step, connect-the-dots system that anyone with the right skills can follow. If one employee leaves, a new one with similar skills can be plugged into the system. Standard operating procedures and employee expertise control the daily operations so the owner is free to work on business development or even take an overdue vacation.

Another way to think about this principle is to reposition your work responsibilities from those of a producer to being the conductor of the orchestra. Your employees are band members in your orchestra, and if they all did their own thing, you'd have a cacophony of noise. It's up to the conductor to bring the different sections of the orchestra together at just the right times so as to create beautiful music.

The business owner does the same thing by directing the various members of his team toward a common goal to produce geometrically growing results. You, as the owner, strategically decide what needs to be done and when, in order to achieve maximum growth, and you delegate to your employees and to your business systems so they produce the desired results.

The ultimate goal is to design your wealth plan so you can leave for three months at a time with the knowledge that your business, real estate, and investment portfolio will all grow in value during your absence. This challenge is not easy. Most businesses fail and the few that "succeed" limp along for years as glorified self-employment.

Probably less than one percent of businesses successfully utilize leverage to attain true freedom.

But when you correctly apply leverage, it's possible for you to geometrically widen the gap between revenues and expenses so that equity grows exponentially rather than arithmetically. I've done it several times, and it's absolutely worth the effort.

It's not easy to do, and I don't want to deceive you by implying that it is. But it's also not any harder than the alternative of working an entire lifetime for financial mediocrity.

IN SUMMARY

You want to accelerate your wealth plan through geometric growth rather than arithmetic growth. The way you seed that growth is by expanding the gap. In paper assets, the gap between income and expenses results in savings for investment; and in business, the gap between income and expenses results in geometric growth of equity as a multiple of earnings.

The greatest potential for expanding the gap is through leveraged growth of income because expense reduction is inherently limited. Income growth is unlimited, and leverage is the accelerator.

EXERCISE: TIME TRACKING 3

This exercise goes the next step beyond categorizing all tasks as either essential or delegable. It's specific to business owners and the goal is to make yourself unessential to the daily operation of the business so you can multiply income growth geometrically.

In this exercise, you assume everything is delegable until it's proven that it's not.

Start by tracking every activity in your day that requires your attention.

For example, every time your team emails you to solve a problem, make a note of that. Every time an employee or virtual assistant asks you a question, note that as well.

In short, every time your work effort is required, treat that as an opportunity to create a system or standard operating procedure to replace your involvement.

For example, in my Financial Mentor business, I used to complete every aspect of publishing every article on the website. Now the team has a standard operating procedure that governs how articles get published, and each person on the team has a specific role. This system has completely replaced my involvement.

The goals of this exercise are: 1) to progressively make yourself unessential for day-to-day operations so you are free to take time off whenever you desire with zero impact on your business; and 2) to work exclusively on business development during the time that you *do* work so you can expand the gap by growing income.

Again, the key to this exercise is tracking absolutely everything *you* do daily in your business and treat those things as a failure of your systems. Try and replace every requirement of your time with some form of leverage until you are completely free.

THE ULTIMATE LEVERAGE

THERE CAN BE NO REAL INDIVIDUAL FREEDOM IN THE
PRESENCE OF ECONOMIC INSECURITY.

– CHESTER BOWLES

I'm trying to be 100% transparent in this book. I don't
want to sugar-coat the instruction with motivational
cheerleading that encourages you to do something
without full awareness.

Leverage may sound great, and it truly *is* amazing when
it's working for you. In fact, you'll pinch yourself because
the results defy intuition. But the truth is, it can be a
tough slog to get there. The goal is valuable, but the
journey can be a lot of work filled with difficult challenges that have to be overcome.

But there's no other choice that makes sense when your
goal is financial freedom. Expectancy math necessitates
that you spend your limited time pursuing *big wins*, and
big wins come through leverage.

Besides, there's no tougher life than working away all
your years to achieve financial mediocrity… or worse.
If you're going to spend all those years working anyway,

then you may as well design your work with leverage so it can lead to outsized wins that result in financial freedom. No other alternative makes sense.

PRINCIPLE 9: FINANCIAL INDEPENDENCE

Life is an adventure; embrace it and live it fully. Who cares if it's hard? Comfort and ease are overrated. Just go for it by playing smart with careful risk management to control losses while pursuing big wins with leverage.

It's literally that simple. Even though the high leverage alternatives that I pursued throughout my career were universally more difficult, there was never really another choice because nothing else made sense for my plan, given my goals. It was the only path worthy of my scarce time.

And this brings us to our final principle: financial independence is the ultimate leverage in life. When you're financially independent, your passive income exceeds your expenses, giving you the freedom to create whatever you want with your life. The bulk of your waking hours that were previously spent earning money, managing money, worrying about money, and spending money are suddenly available for anything you choose, and time is your ultimate scarce resource. Not only that, but you also have the money to do whatever you want with that time. It's that rare combination of both time and money that opens up possibilities for your life. No other goal opens up more possibilities for fulfillment.

Financial freedom gives you the opportunity to serve others without worrying about how much it pays. You can volunteer your time for worthy causes that are personally fulfilling, or you can pursue creative interests in the arts, music, or theatre – even if they never pay you a dime. You can even try that crazy business idea lurking in the back of your head – the one that's personally motivating because it honors your values, but you know it may never pay well.

You can leverage your money to buy the best education available for your children, giving them a solid start in life, and you can free your spouse from having to work for money so you can both pursue a fulfilling life on your own terms.

Financial freedom is the ultimate leverage because it gives you the time and money to live the life you want to live. Nobody ever lay on their death bed wishing they had lived more selfishly or spent more time in the office, so use leverage to free yourself from economic bondage and buy back your time. Once you become financially independent, you can use that time and money to live a full and creative life that gives back to others.

IN SUMMARY

The *9 Principles of Leverage* govern how the *6 Types of Leverage* operate in your wealth plan. They are the "how" and the "why" that drive every strategy you'll use to overcome the resource limitations you face and to break through the constraints that block your wealth growth. By understanding the 9 Principles, you keep yourself from becoming over-worked, distracted, hampered by limited resources, or tempted into risk beyond your tolerance.

It's about getting the fundamentals right so that you're building on a solid foundation. If you're a kid and your goal is to be in the NBA, you need to master the fundamentals. The best players have unbelievable practice discipline to remain at the top of their game. Like an NBA player, you have to focus on drilling the fundamentals of your leverage game. Don't worry about specific outcomes or short-term gains. Play the long game by focusing on the process that reliably produces results and the outcome will be inevitable.

To recap, the fundamental principles of the leverage game are:

1. **Mathematical Expectancy:** Disproportionate payoffs can make you rich if you maximize gains through leverage when you are right and control losses through risk management when you are wrong. Even if you're wrong 9 times out of 10,

or even 99 times out of 100, you can still profit by tilting the payoff portion of the expectancy equation.

2. **Reciprocal Exchange:** Trading your time for money, or trading your money for a product, is limited by your personal resources because that's all you have to exchange. Shift your thinking from the reciprocal exchange model where you trade *time* for dollars, to trading *value* for dollars – because value can be provided in many different ways that free you from personal resource limitations.

3. **Limited Resources:** When you limit yourself to your own resources, you're completely without leverage. You have to rely on your own time, contacts, experience, money, and other resources, and this severely limits your ability to tilt the payoff portion of the expectancy equation.

4. **Time Freedom:** Everyone is allotted the same 24 hours. Successfully applying leverage gives you the freedom to do what aligns with your deepest values so you can pursue fulfillment.

5. **Give Value and Solve Problems:** Business is about solving problems – because people will gladly pay to leverage your solution to their problems. When you master this skill, your growing wealth becomes a measure of how much value you've given to others.

6. **Delegation:** Identify what things have to be done by you, and not by anyone else. Then delegate or partner, so someone else can do the rest. This achieves more, better, faster results and also frees up your time and energy to focus on your strengths and your gifts.

7. **Upfront Costs, Benefits Lag:** There is always an upfront cost that must be paid in terms of time, training, or system development before you can benefit from the lagged results that will be produced.

8. **Expand the Gap:** The objective for all leveraged growth and risk management strategies is to expand the gap between how much you earn versus how much you spend, thus resulting in *equity growth*. In the traditional model, that equity growth translates through savings to become investing for geometric growth; whereas in non-traditional assets like business and real estate, your equity grows geometrically as a multiple of the increased earnings, thus resulting in financial freedom.

9. **Financial Independence:** Life is an adventure. Embrace it and live it fully. Mastering leverage leads to financial freedom, which gives you back your time and opens more possibilities for personal fulfillment.

STRATEGIES:
THE 6 TYPES
OF LEVERAGE

THE 6 TYPES OF LEVERAGE

NO PERSON WILL MAKE A GREAT BUSINESS WHO WANTS TO DO
IT ALL HIMSELF OR GET ALL THE CREDIT.

– ANDREW CARNEGIE

Imagine trying to build a house with only a screwdriver and a hammer. That's what building wealth with only time and financial leverage is like. To build a house you actually want to live in, you also need saws, tape measures, chisels and levels, so you can use the right tool in every situation. Each tool has a specific function, and it must be applied correctly.

Building wealth is just like building your house. You'll need all six leverage tools to overcome the constraints you'll encounter on your journey toward financial freedom – because each tool unlocks a specific limitation that holds you back.

Time and financial leverage are the two most common types of leverage. However, there are four other types of leverage that are less commonly understood but equally valuable. More importantly, each of the six types of leverage delivers a specific solution to a specific type of constraint in your business and financial plans.

For the purposes of our discussion, we'll organize all of the varied leverage tools into the following categories:

1. Financial leverage – Other people's money so you're not limited by your own net worth.

2. Time leverage – Other people's time so you're not limited to 24 hours in a day.

3. Technology and Systems leverage – Other people's technology systems where you set up a scalable business model *once* and your systems can do the work thousands of times.

4. Communications and Marketing leverage – Access other people's audiences through magazines, newsletters, radio shows, podcasts, and databases to communicate with millions of people.

5. Network and Relationship leverage – Expands your reach to include other people's connections so you're not limited to your own.

6. Experience and Knowledge leverage – Employs the expertise of others so you don't have to learn everything yourself.

BOOST YOUR LEVERAGE WITH OVERLAPPING STRATEGIES!

While it's helpful to organize the various leverage tools into a framework built on six categories, the fact is that, in practice, the different types of leverage typically overlap.

For example, my information product business on the Internet uses *technology* to manage and deliver the product, but it's really a form of *knowledge* leverage where I package my *experience* into a scalable business model which then requires *marketing* and *communications* leverage to develop the sales funnels.

Notice how a single business model can apply multiple types of leverage, and how each leverage tool performs a specific function for the business model; yet they are seamlessly interconnected.

The mistake you want to avoid is drawing hard lines in the sand with each category definition. The categories are a useful framework for mentally organizing what would otherwise be an unwieldy collection of tools. They help you understand how to connect the function of each tool to your strategy; however, as you get more accustomed to working with the tools, you'll see how these lines of distinction get blurred.

Always remember that the core principle driving all types of leverage is *to help you do more with less of your own resources by expanding the resources at your disposal.* They are all tools that accelerate your wealth so you can produce faster, greater results.

IN SUMMARY

Think of building your wealth like building a house. Although you may be comfortable wielding a hammer, a hammer isn't appropriate for every situation. You'll need to employ many tools and strategies to accomplish your goals effectively. With leverage, using all six types will help you build the best financial house.

The next few chapters will give you a deep-dive into each type of leverage so you have the tools and strategies necessary to overcome the obstacles that separate you from the financial success you desire.

EXERCISE: 10X YOUR RESULTS

The purpose of this exercise is to break open your thinking from the structured, limited box that all of us tend to get stuck inside.

The idea is for you to create seemingly outlandish goals that you could never achieve when limited to your own resources. Then try and figure out how to actually achieve those crazy goals using leverage.

The cliché slogan (that's actually true) is "when you shoot for the stars, even if you fail, you'll end up on the moon" (which is a pretty amazing achievement).

Your homework is simple. Take whatever goals you have,

multiply them 10 times, and then create serious plans using leverage to actually achieve those new goals.

Try to figure out a realistic way to 10X the results you produce, the income you earn, and your net worth. It will force your mind to incorporate *leverage* to open up new possibilities.

There's simply no other way to achieve a 10X goal. It will shake up your thinking patterns and force new strategies. It will challenge your assumptions and expectations.

So go ahead... how will you 10X your results? Figure out a serious plan to make it happen and see what changes occur in your limiting beliefs.

And then, for extra credit, 10X your 10X goals and repeat the exercise. Push the boundaries. What can you learn?

1 – FINANCIAL LEVERAGE

THE RICH RULE OVER THE POOR,
AND THE BORROWER IS SERVANT TO THE LENDER.

— PROVERBS 22:7

Sean Quinn was the richest man in Ireland, estimated to be worth $6 billion in 2008. By the end of the financial crisis that began that year, he was $3 billion in debt and he declared bankruptcy.

Allen Stanford, founder of the Stanford Financial Group, was worth $2.2 billion before being convicted of operating a Ponzi scheme and losing everything.

Bjorgolfur Gudmundsson built an Icelandic bank to a personal fortune of $1.1 billion in 2008 before filing for bankruptcy in 2009 after the Icelandic banking collapse.

I'm fascinated by stories about people who build vast fortunes, only to quickly lose them. Each story provides a kernel of wisdom regarding what works to build wealth and what can destroy that success. On close inspection, the pattern that emerges is that *leverage* is nearly always the driver behind the rise, and that *inadequate risk management* is the cause of the fall.

The unique characteristic of financial leverage is that

it cuts both ways. It makes the good times great, and the bad times unbearable. It amplifies your return on investment, so when things go south you can get into trouble fast.

Financial leverage places a premium on *risk management skills,* because without them you're just an accident waiting to happen. You must know how to control losses during periods of adversity so you can produce consistently profitable results.

FINANCIAL LEVERAGE VERSUS INVESTING

People often confuse financial leverage with normal investing. Financial leverage is the use of other people's investment capital or debt financing to increase profits. It's putting other people's money to work for you.

This is very different from putting your own money to work for you. For example, investing your money in dividend stocks or bonds is not financial leverage because you're not incurring debt and you have no financing costs to carry.

Yes, it allows you to live off the passive income produced by your capital because it is your *money* that is producing the income, not your *time*, but there is no leverage involved. You're merely putting your investment capital to work so you can make money without regard to how you spend your time.

When you invest your own money, the only cost of capital is the time you took to earn and save it. You have no interest cost and you don't have to repay the money, which is a key distinction. It's very different from borrowed money, which is what we mean by financial leverage.

When you leverage other people's money, you're putting more money to work than you actually own. This creates debt, resulting in a debt-to-equity ratio. The higher the ratio, the greater your financial leverage (and risk!).

Let's say you buy an investment property worth $100,000 by putting 10% down and leveraging the other 90% with mortgage financing. To keep things simple, in this example we'll ignore cash flow and tax considerations so we can isolate the leveraged impact on changes in equity.

If the property increases in value by just 10%, you'll have a 100% return on investment because you only invested $10,000 to control $100,000 in property value. The rest was borrowed. That means a mere 1% increase in property value equals a 10% return on investment. Conversely, if the property drops in value by 10%, you've lost all of your investment. That's the power of financial leverage. When you're leveraged 10:1 it means all changes in equity value are multiplied by 10.

RETURN MUST EXCEED BORROWING COST

The key to profiting from financial leverage is that *your return on investment must exceed the cost of borrowing*. In the example above, where you leverage real estate equity with mortgage financing, you'll increase your profits as long as the real estate returns more than the financing costs net of expenses. The difference between the asset return and the financing costs is your profit.

The obvious implication is that borrowed money should *only* be used to fund an income producing asset, and *never* for consumption. If the money borrowed is used for consumption, that's just extending your spending capability. It's like hiring an employee who gives you massages all day. It might feel good in the moment, but it's not going to grow the business. *Financial leverage should only be used to purchase assets that produce more revenue than they cost.*

For example, let's assume you invest on margin with a 50% maintenance requirement. That means for every $2 invested in equities you only need $1 in cash, so your investment is leveraged 2 to 1. If your equities rise by 100%, your account value will rise by 200% minus financing costs. Conversely, if your equities decline by 50%, your account will decline by 100%, meaning you're wiped out, plus you'll also lose the financing costs.

Notice how financial leverage creates asymmetric returns because you must *subtract* financing costs from the gains, but you also have to *add* financing costs to the losses. The cost of leverage reduces the good times and magnifies the bad times. That's because the carrying cost, or interest on the financing, must get paid *regardless* of the return on investment. So when you get a negative return on investment coupled with interest costs, it's very easy to get in trouble fast.

A great example of this problem is the large number of real estate investors who lost everything during the 2008-2009 economic downturn. The common practice back then was to purchase investment property with a 10% to 20% down-payment and to re-leverage as properties increased in value. In other words, if you bought a house for $100,000 with $10,000 down and it increased 20%, then that $20,000 gain would get reinvested to buy two more $100,000 houses with $10,000 down on each, so you never had more than 10% to 20% in equity. Leverage inflated the bubble by creating more and more demand for investment property as prices rose; but it also led to the destruction of the bubble because a mere 10% to 20% loss in asset value caused a 100% loss of invested capital – resulting in massive foreclosures and forced selling.

Similarly, financial leverage was the cause of both the rise and fall of Long-Term Capital Management in 1998. The firm used highly leveraged strategies in the credit markets, which worked fine... until it didn't. The carrying costs plus leveraged losses buried the fund so fast that it took government intervention to unwind the mess and stabilize the financial markets. They couldn't even sell their losing positions in the market because the entire house of cards collapsed so abruptly.

THE 3 MUST-FOLLOW RULES FOR FINANCIAL LEVERAGE

This section introduces three rules for employing financial leverage in your wealth plan.

RULE 1: AVOID OVER-LEVERAGE

Commodity trading is one of the most leveraged investment strategies. Not surprisingly, more than 90% of all commodity traders end up losing money.

That's not a coincidence.

The contractual leverage built into commodity trading makes it easy to control massive amounts of price change with very little money. If you get on the wrong side of the market just once and your account is undercapitalized (or overleveraged), you're quickly out of the game.

For example, assume you trade sugar futures on the Chicago Mercantile Exchange (CME). Each contract is for 112,000 pounds of sugar. Every 1-point price change in sugar represents $1,120.00 of gain or loss, and the initial margin requirement to control the same contract is roughly the same amount of money. Controlling the price change on 112,000 pounds of sugar with little more than $1,000 (exact margin requirements vary) represents extraordinary leverage. It takes very little price change to wipe out the initial investment.

The rule is simple – the greater your financial leverage, the greater your risk. There's no rule of thumb for what's safe versus not safe. It's simply a sliding scale where less financial leverage is safer and more financial leverage is riskier. The greater your financial leverage, the less room for error you have. You must be sufficiently capitalized to execute your plans through normal, expected setbacks. Never leverage yourself to the point that it puts your survivability in jeopardy.

RULE 2: MANAGE RISK

Financial leverage multiplies your results, which is why it's appealing. It's the kind of leverage that allows you to invest $1,000 today and get $10,000 a few years from now. But because of its enormous multiplication power, your allowable margin for error is much thinner than without it. To manage this risk, you want to put a cap on the downside risks as much as possible just in case a worst-case scenario should strike.

For example, my real estate portfolio was made up of different properties in different states, each held in a separate legal entity, and each building was financed with non-recourse mortgages. That way, if a lawsuit, environmental disaster, or job market change struck one property, the damage would be contained so it didn't impact the other properties, or my personal equity.

Every business and investment strategy must always have a contingency plan for worst case scenarios, and you need to build it into your plan before you *ever* put money at risk. Financial leverage only makes risk management more important because of the much thinner margin for error resulting from multiplying all losses.

RULE 3: MINIMIZE FINANCIAL LEVERAGE DURING DEFLATION

The normal economic reality for investors is inflation. It has been so persistent for most of your lifetime that you might mistakenly assume it's a given, but it's not. Deflation occurs frequently enough that you must be prepared.

Financial leverage is a great strategy when your payment amount is fixed in nominal dollars, but you repay those debts with future, inflated dollars. It's even better when the assets you purchase with leveraged money rise with inflation. In fact, that's exactly how most real estate fortunes have been made.

However, deflation turns that analysis upside down. Asset values decline and you're forced to repay debt in more valuable, deflated dollars. An excellent example is the 2008-2009 real estate market decline that wiped out many investors.

Few people can conceive of deflation's far-reaching impact because of its virtual absence from economic history. The truth is the government wants inflation and generally controls the economy to produce inflation. That's why the dollar has lost 90% of its purchasing power twice since the creation of the Federal Reserve in 1914. Yes, the value of the dollar has declined 90% twice in roughly 100 years, demonstrating the pervasive, powerful force of government-induced inflation.

That's good news for financial leverage because inflation is the economic condition that gives this strategy the greatest probability of success. But it also means you want to be very careful when you see any indications of deflationary risk.

The most common precursor to deflation is an advanced credit bubble. In 2006, anyone in the United States who could fog a mirror could get a 30-year fixed mortgage on almost any size home without even proving income. They were called "liar loans," and through excessive financial leverage they artificially created more demand for housing than people could actually afford. As an avid real estate investor at the time, I chose to do the opposite by selling my investment real estate to reduce my financial leverage, thus controlling my risk exposure to the subsequent deflationary decline.

If you're in the late stages of a credit bubble where deflation is a genuine risk, consider designing your plan to use one of the other five types of leverage described in this book. Be strategic. If the economic environment is unfavorable for financial leverage, risk management tells you to use the other leverage tools that don't cut both ways.

For example, once I had sold all my real estate leading up to the 2007 top, I switched my focus to building FinancialMentor.com using the five other types of leverage that don't carry the same downside risk. It was a conscious decision to manage deflationary economic risk by eliminating financial leverage in real estate. This illustrates a key principle: never get married to any *one* asset class or strategy. Instead, always allocate your capital where the risk/reward is most favorable by avoiding high risk situations. This one strategy has been worth millions to me in my investment career, and it can dramatically improve your investment performance consistency.

IT TAKES MONEY TO MAKE MONEY

Just because I'm cautioning you against financial leverage doesn't mean I don't like financial leverage. When used wisely, it can be an important weapon in your wealth building arsenal – because it's how you overcome the limiting belief that it takes money to make money. The beauty of financial leverage is: if you have a valuable investment opportunity, you can find the capital needed to fund it; you don't need to have your own money.

This is very important because the belief that it takes money to make money is a *dangerous* deception that limits people's wealth plans by closing possibilities.

For example, in an earlier chapter I shared how I acquired 10.2 apartments units using absolutely none of my own money or credit. I worked hard to find a great deal by analyzing investment areas and sorting through more than a hundred properties over a period of months before I could negotiate something that would work. It took skill, discipline, and effort…but zero money.

I know lots of people who've built very profitable internet-based businesses – both in ecommerce and digital publishing – for almost no money out of pocket. Yes, it took a lot of work and they had to develop many skills to succeed, but money was not a factor. What you need is a great idea and the sweat equity to make it happen.

Max Gunther wrote the book "The Very, Very Rich and How They Got That Way," which pulled data from Fortune Magazine's lists of the wealthy that preceded Forbes' now infamous list of the 400 richest people. In 1968, half of the people in Fortune's list inherited their money, but a recent study of the Forbes 400 showed that 69% of the list created their own fortune.

This demonstrates the declining role of inherited wealth over time, as new wealth created by industrious, hard-working entrepreneurs is supplanting old wealth.

Similarly, Amar Bhide wrote, in his book *The Origin and Evolution of New Businesses,* that most of the founders of Inc. 500 companies bootstrapped their business, with a quarter of them starting with less than $5,000, and nearly half with less than $50,000. Think about it. If half of the Inc. 500 was launched with less than $50,000 in starting capital, then clearly money is *not* the obstacle to building wealth.

FINANCIAL LEVERAGE WITHOUT MONEY

Another myth is that the only type of financial leverage is borrowed money, but in fact financial leverage comes in many forms.

For example, derivative financial instruments such as futures contracts and options are highly leveraged investments because they control a much larger amount of underlying assets with a small amount of money than is possible to control through outright ownership.

Futures contracts are legal agreements to buy or sell a commodity or financial instrument at a specified time in the future. They are standardized in both quantity and quality of the commodity to facilitate trading of these contracts on a futures exchange.

The key point is: they are just contractual rights to buy and sell, as opposed to actually buying or selling the underlying commodity itself. This introduces leverage according to the terms of the contract, because the price change in the commodity is controlled by a tiny fraction of the amount of money (margin) that would be required to buy or sell the commodity itself. The contractual obligation is what introduces the leverage, as explained in the earlier example regarding sugar futures.

Options are similar, except the holder has the *right,* but not the *obligation,* to buy or sell the underlying asset at expiration. The futures contract holder is obligated to fulfill the terms of the contract; whereas the option holder literally has the option to exercise his right if his contract is "in the money," meaning the physical price has moved beyond the option strike price. If the option is out of the money at the expiration date, then it expires worthless.

The nuances of leveraged financial contracts create highly specialized investment strategies that require great skill to implement successfully. It's a specialized investment field that should only be accessed if you have proper training and experience. Many claim to sell futures and options courses for beginning investors, but playing with leveraged financial contracts is like playing with fire. The complexity is great enough to burn even experts, and several books would be required to fully explain how they work. They're a highly specialized field of investing that is beyond the scope of this book, which is focused on how to apply leverage to grow your wealth.

What is relevant here is to understand that contractual financial leverage follows the same key principles as discussed in debt leverage above. It cuts both ways by magnifying both the gains and the losses. The difference is, it doesn't require money out of pocket because it's a contractual obligation, not a debt that must be repaid.

HOW OPERATING LEVERAGE MULTIPLIES YOUR PROFITS (AND LOSSES!)

Another form of financial leverage is operating leverage resulting from the cost structure and capital structure of a business.

The cost structure of your business is composed of both fixed and marginal costs. Fixed costs are those costs that don't change when output and sales vary. Variable costs are those costs that change with different levels of output and sales. For example, rent is usually a fixed cost and materials are usually a variable cost.

The higher your fixed costs as a percent of your total cost of goods sold, the higher your breakeven point, which increases both operating leverage and risk. High fixed costs and low variable costs give the greatest operating leverage, resulting in the greatest percentage change in profits, both upward and downward, for any given change in sales volume. A high percentage of fixed costs will magnify the impact of changes in revenue on total profit, which then is multiplied out in equity because the value of any asset is the discounted present value of its cash flow.

In the stock market, you'll see this during economic downturns where companies that experience a small percentage decline in sales will have dramatically reduced profit margins and earnings because the small decline is magnified through operating leverage. For example, a company might require 80% of its sales volume just to support fixed costs, so that all profit comes from the last 20% of sales. That means a 10% drop in sales could reduce profits by a whopping 50%, which might cut the value of the company in half (or worse, depending on market conditions).

ArcelorMittal (symbol MT) is a great example of this problem. Revenues declined by only 15% over a three-year period, but income declined from a positive $2.3 billion to a loss of $2.5 billion over the same time period. This shows how operating leverage can cause disproportionate changes in earnings relative to changes in sales.

What you should notice is how fixed costs increase risk and potential reward, just like other forms of financial leverage. Decreasing fixed costs, thus reducing operating leverage so that costs better match revenue, both reduces risk and potential reward from changes in income. When all costs are variable, the input/output relationship to changes in income is essentially one-to-one. However, the existence of fixed costs amplifies the input/output relationship to greater than one, resulting in operating leverage.

For example, when I bought apartment buildings in the Midwest, the operating leverage was phenomenal compared to the much-more-expensive West Coast. Two-bedroom apartments that rented for $450 per month had fixed operating costs of $300 per month and sold for around 18K to 22K per door because that's all the $150 in leftover income per month could support in mortgage financing.

When the rent for those apartments rose to the $600 to $650 per month range, the value of the building roughly doubled. The fixed expenses for operation remained at $300 per month per unit, but now there was twice as much income left over to support the mortgage payment, causing the building to double in value even though the rents increased by only 30%.

That is an example of operating leverage built into the financial statement of how apartment valuation works. When fixed operating costs equal close to rental value, it means the property is essentially worthless. However, small changes in rental income above fixed operating costs have a magnified impact on property value because of the high operating leverage.

Contrast this high leverage situation with a theoretical San Francisco property that might rent for $2,500 per month and cost a similar $300 per month to operate. The $2,200 per month of leftover income after fixed expenses means there's a lot of revenue to pay the mortgage, which explains why San Francisco property is so expensive. However, when rents rise by the same $200 per month, the increase in property value will only be roughly 10% (because $200 is roughly 10% of the $2,200 in income after expenses). In other words, there's very little operating leverage in this situation.

VALUATION OF APARTMENTS

In general, an investor won't buy an apartment complex if they can't finance the property cost from the rent income. See below how a change in rent of $150 increases the value of a property based on operating leverage.

High Leverage

Rent	Operating Cost	$ for Financing Expenses	Expected Value per Door*	
$450	$300	$150	$20,000	
$600	$300	$300	$40,000	
		Growth of investment from 150 raise in rent		100%

Low Leverage

Rent	Operating Cost	$ for Financing	Expected Value per Door*	
$2,500	$300	$2,200	$293,000	
$2,650	$300	$2,350	$313,000	
		Growth of investment from 150 raise in rent		6.8%

*depends on cap rates, interest rates, and related market factors

This is a simplified example to demonstrate the principle. Of course, no real estate market prices assets exactly this way, but they do follow the principle as demonstrated.

Commodity stocks are another example of operating leverage causing disproportionately large swings in equity. Gold stocks routinely swing 2X to 3X the price change in gold. If gold is up 1%, the gold stock indexes might be up 2% to 3%. That's because the price of gold might be $1500 per ounce but the cost of production for the miner might be $1200. So a $150 move in the price of gold is only a 10% price change, but it equals a 50% increase in profit per ounce for the mining company because of the operating leverage relative to changes in the price of gold.

THE SIMPLE WAY TO BECOME A MILLIONAIRE USING FINANCIAL LEVERAGE

Most Americans correlate wealth with becoming a millionaire. We can probably thank Rich Uncle Pennybags, the Monopoly mascot, for some of this aspiration. If making a million dollars is your goal, let's look at two strategies for achieving millionaire status.

The first strategy has some major flaws, but it's also the traditional financial plan of saving your way to riches.

First, you have to earn the money. Then, you pay taxes on that money. Then, you pay your expenses, and hopefully have a little bit left over to save. With that little bit left over, you invest it to grow. While it's growing, you are paying taxes on that growth. It's a long, slow process with limited growth because of strict mathematical rules.

An alternative but well-proven strategy to become a millionaire is to just borrow a million dollars and invest that money in an asset that produces enough income to pay off the debt. When the debt is paid off, you'll still have the asset and presto, you're a millionaire.

This strategy has several advantages. You immediately begin compounding your wealth on a million-dollar base of positive cash flow assets, such as real estate or business, that then pay the debt back for you. It acts like a forced savings plan where every monthly payment grows equity, plus you benefit from compound growth on a much larger asset base.

It doesn't take a math genius to know that 10% on a million dollar asset you leveraged with debt financing grows equity a lot faster than a 10% return on the $5,000 you were able to save from earned income.

The key concept is: you're immediately working from a much larger base of invested capital, but always remember that this only works *if the asset is cash flow neutral or positive*. That's one of the three rules governing financial leverage – the asset purchased with the borrowed money must return more than the cost of the financing.

It might be an apartment building where the tenants pay the mortgage, or it might be machinery that multiplies revenue for your business, but the asset you leveraged must produce cash flow sufficient to pay the debt back because that's what creates the forced savings plan and allows the compound asset growth to be the gravy on top.

The key principles behind why this strategy works are:

- You're compounding wealth on a much larger base of assets because of leverage through borrowed money.

- You're attaching the investment to a business operation, whether that's a rental housing business or some other business, so there's a source of income to pay the debt.

- Your equity rises as the value of the asset increases and the debt is paid off.

- You also get tax advantages, assuming the interest expense is deductible against income and the asset can be depreciated.

The McDonald's corporation is a classic example of this strategy. Most people think McDonald's is in the hamburger business, but they're really in the real estate business. Hamburgers are just how they pay the mortgage (debt financing leverage). McDonald's occupies some of the most valuable retail real estate locations throughout the world, all paid for by selling fast food.

Corporate bond financing is another example of the same strategy where debt is incurred (financial leverage) to fund the equity growth of the business. As long as the assets created with the debt financing return more than the cost of the debt, the result is accelerated equity growth. The key is: *The return on investment must exceed the cost of capital.*

There are many strategies you can use to leverage borrowed wealth into a personal windfall. Just rethink the generic platitudes and try something new. When analyzing the opportunities, manage your risk exposure carefully and make sure your income creates equity above and beyond the initial investment!

10 MORE WAYS TO GROW YOUR WEALTH WITH FINANCIAL LEVERAGE

If you're not ready to apply the "borrow a million dollars" strategy, there are still many other ways for you to put financial leverage to work in your wealth plan. Consider the following potential strategies to see if any might help you achieve your current wealth goals faster or more reliably:

1. **Lend money**, but get a percent of equity in return, not just interest.

2. **Buy instead of rent**. Rather than rent office space for your business, buy the office space yourself. Use mortgage financing, and have the business pay enough rent to cover the mortgage.

3. **Buy stock on margin.**

4. **Trade commodity futures.**

5. **Buy commodity mining companies**, instead of the underlying commodity, to capture the operating leverage.

6.   **Refinance the equity out of your home** so you can reinvest that equity in additional income-producing real estate. Aim to control more real estate for the same amount of equity.

7.   **Refinance your home so you can redeploy the equity** for investment in a business. (Warning: this increases your risk profile dramatically, so this is *not* a recommendation. It's just an idea to consider.)

8.   **Buy an investment property** using mortgage financing, or find a private lender.

9.   **Build a network** of money partners to finance future real estate purchases.

10. **Lend money to other real estate investors** who have more time and skill to negotiate and manage the deals than you do.

Just to be clear, I'm not recommending that **you** use any of these strategies because many will not be appropriate for your personal situation. This is just a list of potential ideas to consider and to help get your brain thinking about how you could apply various concepts to your own wealth plan. Each is an example of increasing financial leverage to increase potential return, but always remember that they increase risk at the same time.

For the complete list of *101+ Leverage Hacks: A Cheat Sheet for Quickly Implementing Leverage in Your Wealth Plan*, go to https://financialmentor.com/free-stuff/leverage-book.

THE ZEN OF FINANCIAL LEVERAGE: RISK MANAGEMENT

Finally, no discussion of financial leverage is complete without emphasizing the importance of risk management.

Financial leverage both increases potential rewards and decreases the odds of survivability. A highly leveraged business using debt financing has a higher risk of failure than an unleveraged business built on equity alone because the debt must be paid like a fixed cost, effectively creating a form of operating leverage.

Stated another way, the higher the percentage of revenue that flows to profit, or conversely, the lower percentage of revenue that must pay expenses, both marginal and fixed, the safer the business and the lower your risk as an owner.

This is intuitively obvious in the rental real estate business when you own the property free and clear. Your risk of failure is very close to zero because your remaining costs – taxes, insurance, and maintenance – should be a tiny fraction of your rental income. That makes it a very secure way to produce positive cash flow.

The same principles apply to your personal finances. For example, if you have a big mortgage on your home and you have car payments every month because you leveraged up with borrowed money, that means you must earn that much more income to service all that debt before you have anything left over to buy food or fund savings.

Conversely, it's easy to pay your bills and save money when you have no housing costs and no debt. Financial freedom is easier and more secure when your cash flow requirements are lower.

That's why you often see people pay off all their debt as they approach retirement. It increases the reliability of their financial outcome. They're focused on minimizing risk of failure, not maximizing wealth growth, so financial leverage is inappropriate.

DON'T MIX FINANCIAL LEVERAGE WITH VOLATILITY

Another smart rule is to never mix financial leverage with volatile assets because when you're leveraged you have less ability to endure a setback.

For example, conventional fixed rate mortgage financing is generally considered safe in all but extreme cases because real estate is historically not a volatile asset. The rental income stream is reliable enough to support reasonable mortgage financing.

However, you want to avoid high leverage situations when the income stream is volatile. For example, cyclical industries like airlines are highly sensitive to the business cycle because people will spend for vacation air travel in good economic times but stay closer to home when money is tight. This creates volatile earnings which are a dangerous combination with financial leverage because the debt must be repaid regardless of the economic cycle. You want a consistent and reliable cash flow stream to cover the interest payments if you're going to apply leverage to ramp up the equity growth.

Don't get greedy and overleverage. Make sure you're sufficiently capitalized to survive through normal economic setbacks by building a cash cushion. Never leverage yourself enough to put survivability in jeopardy.

IN SUMMARY

In summary, financial leverage is a valuable tool for your wealth plan because it eliminates any excuse for money being an obstacle to financial growth. However, you'll want to apply the following risk management guidelines so you don't get into trouble.

1. Don't over-leverage because the best plans will still experience temporary setbacks, at a minimum. Sometimes worse.

2. Always have an exit strategy to remove leverage and preserve equity so you're prepared with clear action steps should adversity strike.

3. Only leverage assets that provide positive cash flow net of debt service and expenses.

4. Avoid using financial leverage when the income stream supporting the assets is volatile.

5. Financial leverage is most appropriate when your goal is maximum wealth growth but is inappropriate when your goal is security and stability.

6. Avoid financial leverage in deflationary economic environments.

Financial leverage used wisely can make you rich. If you apply this tool with skill and careful risk management, it can produce extraordinary results. However, it can cause a financial disaster when applied incorrectly. It's like pouring gasoline on a fire. It will turbo-charge results, but it can also turn a little problem into a big problem fast. It's the only form of leverage that cuts both ways, so be careful.

If you'd like to learn more about risk management and how to apply it to leverage you can take the companion mini-course *Risk Management: How To Make More By Losing Less* (https://financialmentor.com/educational-products/risk-management-course).

EXERCISE: FINANCIAL LEVERAGE IN REAL ESTATE

Here's a quick exercise, using three different scenarios, that will deepen your understanding of how financial leverage magnifies both investment return and risk.

Assume you invest in a $200,000 property with mortgage interest rates at 7%, and a 5% annual property value appreciation rate.

In *the first scenario*, you pay cash for the property so you own it free and clear. Using the compound interest calculator here – https://financialmentor.com/calculator/monthly-compound-interest-calculator – you'll see that the property is worth roughly $542,000 in 20 years, resulting in a compound return on investment of 5%.

In *the second scenario*, you apply financial leverage using a traditional 30-year fixed rate, fully amortizing mortgage of $180,000 with a 10% down-payment. Using the mortgage calculator with amortization schedule (found at https://financialmentor.com/calculator/mortgage-payment-calculator-amortization-schedule), after 20 years of payments your remaining balance would be $103,000 with a loan balance reduction of $77,000. That means your equity in the house is roughly $440,000 on your initial investment of $20,000. Even after subtracting the discounted present value of your payment stream of $1,197.54 for 20 years, the remaining equity represents a much higher return on investment than in scenario 1 because of the financial leverage.

In *the third scenario*, you decide to get more aggressive by re-leveraging the equity in your house every five years over the same 20-year period, by buying additional properties, assuming the same 10% down and 5% growth. For example, at the end of five years you'd have roughly $60,000 in equity to re-leverage into a $600,000 property. Rinse and repeat every five years and you'd have four properties valued at roughly $6.7 million, for an extraordinary return based on your initial investment of just $20,000.

Accelerate the re-leveraging interval to every two years and the ending value jumps to $56 million; or lengthen the interval to every 10 years and it drops to less than $2 million.

However, always remember that financial leverage cuts both ways. Using the same three examples, a 30% downturn in property values six years into the holding period wouldn't faze the cash buyer in scenario one, would destroy all the equity in scenario two, and would give scenario three a negative net worth and likely destroy a lifetime of wealth building. The greater the financial leverage, the greater the risk of failure and the thinner your margin for error.

So how much financial leverage fits your wealth plan and is consistent with your goals? Is it scenario 1, 2, or 3 (or something in between)?

2 – TIME LEVERAGE

My philosophy is to always find the smartest people
you can. Hire people smarter than you.

– Donny Deutsch

Time is limited. You can't make more of it. You can't
save it. You spend it every minute you're alive, and
you never get to know how much of it you have left.

The only question is: What do you spend your precious
time on? Everyone gets the same 24 hours in a day, and
we all have the same final destination when time ends.
The countdown to that destination never stops, until
it does.

There's no question time is your most precious resource;
yet, isn't it amazing how most of us treat time as if we're
blessed with an unlimited supply?

How will you maximize the value of your time given
that it's scarce? In this chapter you'll learn how to
leverage time to help you realize your full potential in
this lifetime.

WHAT'S YOUR TIME WORTH?

Knowing the value of your time is important because it affects what you spend it on. Your hourly rate shows you which activities you should personally complete and which activities should be eliminated or leveraged away through outsourcing because their value is below your hourly rate.

The reason you're not making as much money as you'd like is because you haven't increased the value of your *time* to the level you need in order to make that much money.

How you think about your time and how you value it will largely determine the financial results you produce with that time, because if you don't value your time, nobody else will either.

4 REASONS DELEGATION IS YOUR NEW BEST FRIEND

One way to increase the value of your time is through time leverage. It's the principle of delegating tasks to others so *their* time is completing the task rather than *your* time.

There are four main benefits to time leverage:

1.   You get more done faster.

2. You get stuff done without using any of your own time, thus buying you freedom.

3. You get lower value (but still necessary) activities done by someone else so you can focus on just the highest value activities that will accelerate progress and profits.

4. You disconnect your income from your limited time so it can grow beyond an hourly rate.

Leveraging time is an important skill to develop because it's a mistake to try to do everything yourself. Businesses hire employees because no boss has all the skills and time necessary to perform every function in the business.

Unfortunately, most people don't think in terms of time leverage, and this causes them to work in a linear fashion trading time for money. When money gets tight, they work harder or they work longer hours.

The goal of time leverage is to release your income growth from the boundaries of time. With time leverage, the amount of income you can create is limitless. As long as each increment of time leveraged (through an employee or business system) accrues excess value to you, then the more time you leverage, the more money you'll make.

Time leverage can also save you time by replacing your work time with someone else's services, thus giving you more personal time. For example, you can use time leverage to buy back time from mundane activities like mowing the lawn, shopping, or cleaning the house so you can spend it on activities more important to your fulfillment, like family, friends, personal growth, and travel.

There's nearly always someone who is better at a specific skill or more qualified than you. Your goal is to identify those high value tasks that only *you* should complete, which is that rare intersection of activities where your unique skill set overlaps high value tasks that absolutely require your personal genius. Everything else should be delegated so you can focus your limited time where it has the greatest value to move your wealth forward.

For example, if you're a real estate investor, it might make sense in the early years to manage your own properties when cash flow is tight and you need to learn the landlord business. But at some point, your real estate business will cross a threshold where time spent on the minutiae of paperwork, leasing, and maintenance distracts you from higher value activities like networking for deal flow, making offers, arranging financing, and completing due diligence.

Stated another way, landing one smart deal because you were focused on high value tasks could pay for all your property management and overhead in perpetuity. Unfortunately, too many real estate investors miss that opportunity because they're working on the plumbing.

That's why I don't clean my house, mow my lawn, or maintain my cars. I'm actually really competent at those activities, and I could save a bunch of money if I did it all myself. The problem is I don't enjoy any of those tasks, and others can do them better than I can. More importantly, they're not the highest and best value for my time because I can make more than the cost of those services by dedicating the same time to growing my business.

In other words, I don't hire help because I can afford it. I hire help because it makes me wealthier and happier.

WHY FRUGALITY IS A LOW-LEVERAGE STRATEGY

This is one of the challenges to the frugality path to wealth that's popularized by many of the FIRE (financial independence retire early) blogs on the internet.

Their strategic focus is nearly always frugality utilizing the conventional unleveraged financial plan built around spending less and saving more from earned income: the "spend less – save more" framework. There's nothing wrong with this strategy except that it's extremely limiting because you can end up working as hard at saving money to keep expenses down as you would just making the money in the first place. It's a low-leverage strategy that's totally acceptable if your values align with a belief structure that finds minimalism satisfying.

However, an equally valid alternative is what I like to call "Fat Fire." It's built around an alternative planning framework based on making more through leverage and losing less through risk management: the "make more, lose less" framework. Again, there is no right/wrong judgment in this discussion. It has absolutely nothing to do with claiming that one path is better than another. Instead, it's about expanding awareness of the tradeoffs in each approach to financial freedom, so you can decide what best fits your values and life goals as you design your wealth plan. One approach is low leverage and limiting; the other approach is high leverage and unlimited.

The key is to make a conscious choice that fits your individual needs. Either path can deliver financial freedom, but the process and the outcomes will be radically different.

HOW PRODUCTIVE IS YOUR PRODUCTIVE TIME?

Another important point about time leverage is how success is created at the margin. Typically, 80 to 90 percent of your time is used just to get by in life, leaving just 10 to 20 percent to produce something truly extraordinary with the little time remaining.

In other words, the daily requirements of life, like sleeping, bathing, eating, preparing meals and running errands, chew up much of your life. Talking on the phone, checking your web stats, clearing email, organizing your desk, and creating social media updates are all maintenance activities that distract you from what I'll call "productive time." The truth is, most of your day is spent on maintenance activity, leaving little productive time to move your life forward.

I'm not saying these maintenance activities should be

eliminated entirely because they're an essential part of a full and healthy life. Instead, I'm simply creating a clear distinction about what productive time is and how relatively few hours actually get dedicated to real productivity.

The only time you're "productive" is when you do the work that directly leads to your goals, or you leverage someone else's time to do the same. Productive time directly grows your business and revenue. This includes product development, marketing systems, sales, and creating business systems that further leverage time. In real estate, it might be analyzing deal flow, making offers, arranging financing, and completing due diligence. The exact activities that qualify as productive time will vary from business to business.

Finding productive time requires focus; otherwise maintenance activities will expand to fill all your available time. *You must prioritize productive time or you won't have any. It doesn't happen on its own.*

This problem is illustrated by studies of Fortune 500 CEO's showing that the total productive time in their day is something close to *30 minutes*, depending on the actual research study.

This leads to two startling conclusions that can change your life and change what you're able to produce with your scarce time resources.

The first principle is that success is created at the margin.

For example, one of my rules from coaching clients on wealth building is: if you want to know how long it will take for someone to achieve any goal, just look at how much of their time they dedicate to that goal. Notice how similar that is to our definition of productive time.

The unfortunate truth is you likely have very few productive hours in each day to dedicate to achieving your goals. That's why recapturing a wasted hour here and there by redirecting it to productive use is so valuable. You're not just adding one hour to an already long 10-hour day for a 10% incremental improvement. Instead, adding one productive hour could literally *double* your productive time, because your long day only has one other productive hour in it. That's why *success exists at the margin of time.* Doubling your productive time by one hour might 2X or 4X your results, which could be life changing. In a moment, you'll learn six strategies to help you do this.

The second key principle about productive time is how business systems, and developing standard operating procedures for employees as a business system, can be the most productive time of all because that's how time literally multiplies itself.

HOW EMPLOYEES AMPLIFY YOUR PRODUCTIVE TIME

But before I explain employer time leverage, I need to make a key distinction between *tasks* versus *processes* because one is dramatically more productive than the other.

When you leverage employee time, you're investing in your business to produce an outcome that has greater value than it costs you. You're paying to get something in return. It's an investment, so like all investments you want to maximize gains and minimize losses. You do that by focusing on *process*.

Your goal is to progressively advance your productive time from **working in** the business on projects and tasks, to **working on** the business by developing systems and processes that *increase your time leverage*.

Systems are created for business activities that recur on a regular basis – a process that repeats over and over again. Whereas *projects* are one-offs, goal-oriented activities with a specific beginning and end.

For example, when I spend two days of work training an employee on a business system that she will implement half-time for the next two years, I've literally bought a year of productivity for two days of my time. So it's an example of a high-leverage activity.

Notice how different that is from asking an employee to complete a specific project. Delegation of single tasks leverages time, but the effect is linear. It's limited because once the task is completed, you then have to repeat the cycle by identifying the next project, setting new metrics for success, and training the employee for the next limited, specific outcome. Once that project is completed, you do it again and again, with each project requiring a chunk of your time.

However, delegating an entire operating procedure so the employee can work independently on an ongoing basis is highly leveraged. That means your goal in time leverage is to identify *work processes* that can deliver a constant stream of value.

The more you can delegate and train employees in work processes, treat them well, and give them the space to express their true talents, the more leverage you'll see for your efforts. The key is to properly match the job requirements with the knowledge and skills the employee brings to the table so as to achieve maximum productivity.

Of course, this only works when your employees share your vision and values and possess a strong internal will to do better, to contribute more, to stay focused on results, and to grow in efficiency. Employees must have this emotional intelligence or their value will be limited.

The idea is to always *hire up* by finding people smarter and better than you for any specific skill set, because they'll get more done and save you time. Be ruthlessly selective upfront because you either put the time into getting the right person, or you put in the time later when you get rid of the wrong person and then try to find and train the right person all over again.

As team leader, you must be constantly vigilant that everyone is contributing forward momentum to your team to maximize the value of time leverage. One bad apple can hurt the output and morale of the entire team.

Winners like to work with other winners, so the wrong people will cause heartache and frustration for the whole team, potentially resulting in your best people leaving to find a stronger team they can attach to and rise with.

That means you must be vigilant to make sure everyone you leverage pulls their weight by delivering unique contributions to the team goals. Anyone that hinders the growth of the entire organization should be swiftly removed and replaced. It's better to find new leaders than risk losing your best people because of a negative team member.

SYSTEMS AUTOMATION: THE ULTIMATE TIME LEVERAGE STRATEGY

Finally, the last step in time leverage doesn't involve anyone's time at all because you replace human time with automated business processes that run 24/7 for many years into the future.

Setting up automated business processes can deliver the greatest leverage of all. For example, I developed an automated opt-in procedure for my website at Financial Mentor.com that builds relationships by delivering value to my new visitors. The automation provides huge leverage by converting them to subscribers and later to customers without me personally sending a single email. This system does the work of many employees at a fraction of the cost by running 24/7 with unlimited scalability. You can test it for yourself here: https://financialmentor.com/free-stuff/free-ebooks; or you can surf the site and notice all the different ways you are incentivized to subscribe. There are free courses, books, calculators, PDF downloads, resource guides, and other incentives – all operating 100% on autopilot to give value by building trust and relationships with new subscribers. It's an entire *business system.*

Compare that to producing a presentation that I might deliver one time to a single group of people. They both qualify as leverage, but the sales presentation is a project that gives a *linear* return on my time because it must be repeated over and over, with each instance consuming more time to deliver only linear value. Both sell products and both are productive time, but the *project* is limited while the *process* is highly leveraged.

6 PRACTICAL TIME LEVERAGE STRATEGIES

Depending on your personal situation, one or more of the following strategies may accomplish the time leverage you need.

1.   **Hire an assistant**. In your business, outsource the mundane tasks that you don't enjoy so as to free up your time and allow you to focus on the projects that specifically require your unique skills.

2.   **Hire an employee**. Then delegate tasks to them.

3.   **Hire a freelancer**. Don't need a part-time or full-time employee? Delegate a task through Upwork or any other international, online, freelancing network.

4.   **Use an online calendar and scheduling system** so clients can book their own appointments and manage their schedule independently without you having to invest your time or effort. I use https://appointlet.com, but there are many acceptable alternatives including https://calendly.com. My online appointment system automatically syncs to my calendar at zero cost, and the

only thing I do is update availability once every three months. The time savings of not having to coordinate calendars through multiple emails to schedule each appointment is extraordinary.

5. **Conduct meetings online.** Skype, Zoom, and other virtual conference rooms are almost free compared to the huge cost and time required to drive or fly out to meet someone in person.

6. **Use webinar software** to deliver an on-demand seminar or program. You present it once, and then thousands of people see it without any additional work on your part.

These are just six examples of the many potential time leverage strategies included in my free, downloadable list that shows you more than 100 ways to get faster, greater results by increasing the leverage in your wealth plan. You can get instant access to this regularly updated and constantly growing list here: https://financialmentor. com/free-stuff/leverage-book.

HOW TO PRIORITIZE YOUR TIME FOR MAXIMUM LEVERAGE

The way you break the time-for-money boundaries is by advancing from linear to leveraged productivity. It's how you get more work done and create more profit without working more... or maybe even working less.

The steps to progressively increase the value of your time through leverage are:

1. Increase the proportion of truly productive time in your day. You want to recover those marginal hours that will literally double and triple your total productivity.

2. Delegate projects so you can multiply the amount of time working toward your goals, thus accelerating your progress.

3. Increase your time leverage from linear project leverage to the more valuable process leverage by systematizing all functions in your business, and then isolating those functions that don't need your active involvement and delegating them.

4. Further increase leverage by replacing human time from the production equation with scalable business system automation.

The goal is to progressively advance your time leverage skills, first by increasing productive time and then further leveraging that productive time from linear project leverage to geometric system leverage.

Time spent developing *systems* is some of the most highly leveraged because it's not about working smarter. It's about building a system to replace yourself within your own business or job, and that brings you closer to freedom, which is the real goal.

IN SUMMARY

Time is a limited commodity. Every man and woman is allotted the same 24 hours per day. Only by leveraging automation and the time of others can you truly accomplish your financial goals. Whether you delegate, hire, automate, or drop unneeded tasks from your to-do list, the benefit of freeing that bandwidth is exponential. You can use that time to create and build the next step in your wealth plan, and ultimately reach the financial freedom you desire.

EXERCISE: CALCULATE THE VALUE OF YOUR TIME.

Step 1: What is your annual income goal?

Step 2: Calculate the number of hours you want to work by multiplying *the number of hours per day that you want to work* by *the days you want to work per week* by *the number of weeks you want to work per year*. This product will give you the total hours you want to work to achieve that income level.

Step 3: Divide the total hours into the income goal to get your hourly rate.

Step 4: Divide 60 into your hourly rate to get the value of every minute in your day.

Now that you have that number, what are you going to do with that time? Are you going to play video games, watch network television, or surf the internet? Is it worth your time?

What's the most important thing you can do with your time to maximize your fulfillment?

3 – TECHNOLOGY & SYSTEMS LEVERAGE

IF YOU CAN'T DESCRIBE WHAT YOU'RE DOING AS A PROCESS,
YOU DON'T KNOW WHAT YOU'RE DOING.

– EDWARD DEMING

Your goal with systems leverage is to convert all activities required to run your business into standardized *processes* so they automatically deliver your business's value proposition without any input from you. The result is a scalable, efficient, profitable business that also gives you time freedom.

Systems leverage is interconnected with time leverage because you pay the price of time upfront to create the system, but the *system* does the work down the road without requiring your time.

I define a system as a set of procedures that produces consistent results for the business regardless of the contractor, employee, or technology using it. Think of it like the recipe you'd use to bake a cake, describing the exact steps to follow and the exact ingredients to use for each step in the process.

There are two primary benefits to systemizing:

1. **Systems take the unknowns out of the business process by standardizing it into a work flow that produces a reliable output.** For example, you may not like McDonald's restaurant food, but you always know exactly what you'll get regardless of which location you go to, because the business systems standardize every detail. Similarly, banks systemize every aspect of depositing and withdrawing funds, or accessing your safe deposit box, because they have a responsibility to assure the secure management of people's money.

2. **Systems leverage your knowledge into a scalable, efficient process that reduces cost and, most importantly, gives you time freedom.**

Systems leverage is the difference between building a business asset that you own versus having a business that owns you. The goal is to design your business so the work gets done without your input by systemizing it in every possible way.

THE 3 STAGES OF SYSTEMS LEVERAGE THAT EVERY BUSINESS MUST GO THROUGH

You should expect to progress through three stages of increasing sophistication as you implement systems leverage:

1. Process map repetitive tasks into standard operating procedures so that reliable, high-quality, efficient results are produced every time with a minimum of mistakes.

2. Integrate technology leverage so that you start replacing human labor with machine labor, further reducing costs and improving results.

3. Design audit controls with checks and balances into your systems so they're self-correcting.

Examples of the types of systems you'll use to better manage your business and real estate assets include:

- A **marketing system** that delivers a continuous flow of qualified prospects.

- A **lead generation system** that builds a database of prospects for your business.

- A **conversion system** that nurtures all prospect relationships until they're ready to buy.

- A **sales system** that converts prospects into customers by collecting payment.

- An **onboarding system** that welcomes each new customer.

- A **product delivery system** that delivers the value to the customer.

- A **training system** for employees and contractors.

- An **accountability system** that monitors all the other systems and shows you when any system breaks down, similar to how a warning light on your car dashboard tells you to repair minor failures.

In short, you want to create a system for every repetitive activity in your business, which just happens to include most of the activities that occur in the business.

PROCESS MAPPING TODAY TO FREE YOUR TIME TOMORROW

The best way to begin systemizing is through process mapping.

You start by documenting every business activity that repeats so you can map it into a standard operating procedure or business system. This leverages your knowledge into a repeatable system, or way of doing things, that can be used by contractors and employees.

Process mapping works by breaking each repetitive work process down to its essential elements and connecting those elements with arrows or lines in a visual, intuitive design to show the most efficient flow of activity. Each process has a...

- Beginning
- Action

- Decision
- Action
- Ending

PROCESS MAPPING

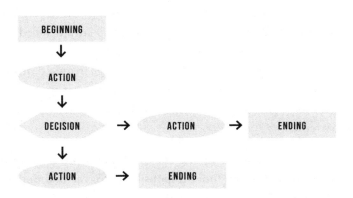

Notice the simplicity. Because the beginning and end of the process only occur once, you're actually left with only two elements to every process: decisions and actions. This framework reduces task completion down to its essential elements, so it's easy to optimize how you complete each work flow by standardizing decisions and eliminating unnecessary actions.

This improves efficiency because the first time you do anything is the most difficult. You have to figure it out and fumble through mistakes and missteps. The next time you do something you'll be more efficient, but your learning curve will still be steep. That's the best time to begin fleshing out the Standard Operating Procedure (or SOP) for that process, because you still have beginner's eyes that will help you explain every detail of every action and decision required – so a beginner with no experience can complete the same task efficiently and without error.

As you continue to implement the procedure, you'll refine your knowledge with nuances, allowing you to continue improving the SOP until it's sufficiently detailed that an employee can operate it from day one without training. At this point, all the knowledge required to complete the task is built into the system, so that anyone with the right qualifications can produce the same quality result.

The final step in converting the SOP into a permanent business asset is to transfer responsibility for maintaining and improving the SOP to the employee operating it, so it's always kept up to date. In other words, working from the SOP and keeping it up to date becomes a primary employee responsibility defined right in their job description.

You may have to navigate employee resistance toward standard operating procedures because some employees may initially believe that creating or maintaining SOPs will mean less job security. But that's not the case. You have to educate employees so they understand that SOPs help make the company more successful, which in turn increases their job security (assuming they perform their job well). The more they contribute to the company, the more they'll get back and the greater their job security.

It also helps when you build SOPs into the employee review process. If employees are told they are expected to maintain a SOP, they'll be more likely to stick with it and update it.

The goal of a SOP is to never reinvent the wheel because reinvention wastes valuable resources. Instead, you want to include all the knowledge required to complete every repetitive task in a standard operating procedure – so that knowledge is never lost and mistakes are never repeated.

This is critically important for three reasons:

1.   Your business will waste valuable resources and operate at less than peak efficiency if you have flawed processes.

2.   Standard operating procedures are what make a business run efficiently to produce reliable, high-quality results every time. Systems convert complexity into efficient order by transferring the knowledge of the owner and key employees into procedures that operate without dependence on any key individual.

3.   You can never gain freedom from your business unless it's operated by systems so effective they don't require your input. You want to treat every task that crosses your desk as a *failure* of your business systems. The amount of your involve-

ment in daily business operations is a measure of the quality of your systems.

PROCESS MAPPING TOOLS TO MAKE YOUR LIFE EASIER

While I like the process map diagram to explain how to design business systems, the truth is I'm a big fan of keeping things as simple as possible. That's why my favorite alternative tool for mapping workflows is to simply outline them in word processing software like MS-Word or a Google Doc.

The reasons I prefer word processing software are:

- Accessibility and ease of editing the workflow in a document format.

- Ability to add instructional notes to each decision and action in the process. The result is a complete, stand-alone training document that can easily be adapted to a checklist format by the employee.

- Outline formatting using numbered bullet points because it creates an intuitive, sequential flow to the process.

You can get two free sample SOP's that we use at Financial Mentor at https://financialmentor.com/free-stuff/leverage-book. They will give you tangible examples and a template for preparing your own SOP. Just follow the instructions on the page and the system will send the files to you instantly.

However, just because I like using *outline docs* doesn't mean you should do the same. Instead, use whichever tool works best for you and your team. Some people prefer mind-mapping; others like visual workflows; and I just happen to like the simplicity of a bullet point outline.

There's no right or wrong answer; however, keep it simple and choose a format that's easy to edit because the process must adapt in real time as the work gets streamlined with new learning. If you can't quickly edit the workflow, it will become dated and inaccurate, thus defeating the whole purpose.

For example, at Financial Mentor, nearly every function of the business – from social media management to article posting to customer engagement – has a standard operating procedure. And every time we learn something new that results in a change, we immediately update that standard operating procedure. The overall result is an Operations Manual that governs how the entire business runs, so I can focus on creating the books, courses, and educational articles that drive the business forward.

One measure of the quality of these procedures is how I'm able to take extended trips, up to two months at a time, while the business grows, problems get solved, and nearly all issues get handled with close to zero communication from me. Each team member acts independently, communicates with others, and copies me on emails when relevant. But because of the business systems, everything happens flawlessly while I'm out of reach or taking a family vacation. Your objectives should be similar if you want to maximize your freedom.

MAKING MONEY SHOULD BE BORING

Great systems convert making money into a boring routine...and that's a good thing.

Creativity occurs when you're developing your business model, but profits occur when you convert it into a formula that repeats over and over. Standardize and systemize. Your goal is to detail every function of the business to the point that it bores you, so then your only remaining task is to do creative work that takes the business to the next level.

For example, when I ran an immensely profitable hedge fund, every aspect of the business got systemized. All investment management decisions were determined by mathematical and statistical risk management systems. No human interpretation or emotions were ever allowed to enter the investment decision process. It was 100% formula driven.

All investment management and accounting systems were updated following a strict data management process with error-tracking routines. All accounting followed a pre-prescribed monthly process with a structured pattern for completing every task. Even the monthly newsletter to investors was standardized.

Because all the business admin functions were automated with rigorous discipline, I was able to run the entire company working less than two hours per day, except on the first day of each new month when the accounting had to be done and the investor newsletter had to be written. That day required a full eight hours of work. It was a wonderfully simple business model until the partners grew apart and decided to sell the business to pursue other dreams.

However, if every function of the business hadn't been standardized, the result would have been complexity and problems. For example, the monthly accounting used to take days to complete before I built the systems. Worse yet, weeks were spent every year trying to solve errors and manually correct problems – before we created a system that caught and corrected them in real time. Similarly, investment management would have been all but impossible without the mathematically disciplined risk management systems because human emotion would have invaded the decision process causing damaging errors.

The key to making automation this efficient is ensuring that your business systems run the business, not *you*. The owner must lead the effort by referring all questions and new innovation to the standardized operating procedures, so employees and contractors get a clear, consistent message that the operations manual must operate the business.

You want all procedures and practices determined by the operations manual – not the owner or key employee – because that's what frees your business from your time and knowledge. It allows you to train new people easily, outsource functions when needed, and continually improve performance.

Everyone must know what processes they're responsible for and how their responsibilities relate to the overall business. Nobody should wing it. A well-run business is synonymous with having an agreed-upon process for nearly everything.

MAKING TECHNOLOGY WORK FOR YOU

The next step in systems leverage after mastering standardized operating procedures is to add *technology systems* so that tasks are completed by machines instead of humans.

Technology has a long, proven history of delivering speed and efficiency improvements. For example, technology has evolved transportation over the years from walking and riding horses to bicycles, then cars and boats, and more recently bullet trains and supersonic airplanes. Each generation of technology improves the speed and efficiency of transportation.

You can see a similar trend in communication. It began with person-to-person conversation, then advanced to telephone and radio, which then developed into television, and has now progressed to email, texting, webinars, podcasts, live chat, and YouTube.

Personal computers, smart phones, and the internet have combined with SaaS (or Software as a Service) vendors to provide affordable technology tools you can leverage as a small entrepreneur. A home-based business can now compete on equal footing with a Fortune 500 company because both the software and hardware are so powerful and affordable.

For example, local musicians now produce studio quality recordings using nothing more than a laptop, a few microphones, cords, and editing software. Before this home technology existed, they were limited by the barriers of cost prohibitive studio time and expensive sound engineers only accessible through a big record label.

A similar revolution has occurred in publishing. New York publishing houses can't compete against the flood of quality books from self-published authors armed with nothing more than a laptop, an internet connection, and access to direct-to-consumer marketing channels like Amazon.

Technology has flattened the playing field by eliminating barriers to entry for the little guy. Software and hardware companies are producing off-the-shelf business systems that allow the home entrepreneur to compete at any level. The result is that bigger is no longer better.

However, all of this access to technology tools has a downside risk as well. As you learned in time leverage, *you* shouldn't do everything yourself, even if you have affordable access to all the technology tools required to complete the job.

You have to be careful not to get buried in technology by balancing time leverage principles with technology leverage possibilities. In the end, your ultimate limit is *time*, and all technology requires time to learn, set up, and maintain.

HOW TECHNOLOGY REVOLUTIONIZES BUSINESS SYSTEMS

The goal behind technology leverage is simple: replace human function with machine function wherever possible to lower costs and increase efficiency.

It's business systems taken to the extreme when you process map operations with such refined detail that a machine can complete them. You pay a one-time, fixed cost to purchase and set up the machine function – that has almost no marginal cost and infinite scalability; runs 24 hours a day, seven days a week; never charges you overtime, never gets sick, and never takes holidays. Examples include:

- Using a website as a content marketing machine to attract targeted traffic to your business on autopilot.

- Providing an electronic, printable brochure on-line that can be downloaded rather than printed and mailed.

- Autoresponders to build relationships with new subscribers by delivering value through an educational course.

- Downloadable eBooks instead of printing and mailing a physical book.

- Print-on-demand physical books that have no inventory costs because you no longer have to stockpile cases of books in a warehouse.

- Autoresponders to handle routine clerical and communications functions.

- Automated order placement and credit card processing instead of a call center with a person on the phone.

- Automated accounting so all sales and expense data transfer automatically to the accounting system without manual input.

- Digitally sign and attach files to emails to deliver documents instantly at zero cost, compared to the expense and delay of printing and overnight shipping a physical document.

- Automated file backup to the cloud instead of warehousing boxes of paper.

- Online calendar and scheduling systems so coaching clients and podcast hosts can book their own appointments independently without any time or effort required from you. In my case, this online appointment system syncs automatically to my calendar at zero cost, so the only thing I do is update my availability once every three months by carving out my vacation and personal time. The time savings of not having to coordinate calendars through multiple emails to schedule each appointment is extraordinary.

- Electronic files can deliver standardized responses to frequently asked questions and routine procedures, so you can just copy and paste the response in seconds rather than manually writing an original each time.

- Free online newsletters to communicate the same message to hundreds of thousands of people for almost no cost, compared to the old per-unit expense required for physical printing, stuffing envelopes, postage, and snail-mail.

- Online membership sites that deliver 24/7 secure access to a course from anywhere in the world, compared to the expense and inconvenience of manufacturing binders, CD's, and videos, and then warehousing, boxing, and shipping all the material.

These are just a few examples that demonstrate how you can leverage technology into automated business systems to lower costs, increase scalability, and save time.

For the complete list of *101+ Leverage Hacks: A Cheat Sheet for Quickly Implementing Leverage In Your Wealth Plan*, go to https://financialmentor.com/free-stuff/leverage-book.

CHECKS AND BALANCES TO REDUCE RISK

An advanced form of systems leverage occurs when you build feedback loops into your systems to improve and monitor results. This includes adding checks and balances as well as creating performance metrics.

The reality is that each system introduces an inherent risk that something could go wrong if left unchecked. That risk requires you to compartmentalize and control exposure to an acceptable level should the worst happen.

For example, if you have one employee keeping the books, you want someone else responsible for collecting and reporting revenue, and a third person responsible for audit. This way, no one person has end-to-end control over the revenue side of your business, a state-of-affairs that could allow them to "cook the books" and run off with the money.

Similarly, if you have one employee who supervises all employees with end-to-end control, you will want to give all the other employees direct access to you so they can report if anything is seriously wrong that merits the attention of you, the owner.

In other words, you always want to maintain accountability, with checks and balances built into the system. That way, you avoid the risk of a problem developing and being unmonitored and uncorrected, thus growing into a bigger problem.

In addition to checks and balances, another useful tool is *performance metrics* because they tell you quickly when something is wrong. You can't improve what you don't measure. That's why you need quantifiable metrics, directly connected to the goal for that system, that determine minimum acceptable levels of performance.

For example, at FinancialMentor.Com, all revenue is connected to traffic and conversion statistics. The formula for the business is

TRAFFIC * CONVERSION = PROFIT

The more traffic, the greater the number of new subscribers, book sales, course sales, advertising, and affiliate revenue. So the primary metric is *traffic*, and the secondary metric is *conversion*.

Conversely, it never makes sense to focus on book sales or advertising revenue directly. Instead, focus on the metrics that determine what sales will be – in this case, traffic and conversion. Focus on the *cause* so you can measure and improve it. The effect will take care of itself.

This type of performance measurement removes all ambiguity from employees and contractors by clearly defining the objective for the system they're working toward optimizing. It makes it clear to everyone in the business what the proper focus should be.

INCREASE SCALABILITY FOR MAXIMUM PROFITS

How scalable is your business?

The quickest way to tell is to note all the places in your business where *your time* is required. If there is work that needs your involvement, and that can't be turned into a system, it's going to be a clog that reduces the scalability of your business.

Using Financial Mentor as an example, the clog to growth is getting the ideas out of my head into written form – articles, books, and courses – because this can't be delegated. I'm the only one who can do it because they are my ideas and the core value proposition to the educational products. This is a fundamental flaw that limits the business model because everything else – marketing, conversion, traffic generation, social media, sales, and customer service – can be delegated and systemized. Everything is scalable except my writing time.

Your goal is to develop your wealth plan so it's not limited by your personal resources because that limits scalability, which is essential for producing big results that tilt the payoff component of your expectancy equation. Scaling requires systems leverage. You can't do it all yourself.

Realtors are a good example of the scaling problem. Listing and showing a property is a personal service requiring the personal attention of your realtor. The client rightfully expects the realtor herself to help price and list the house. That's why the client hired the realtor; therefore, it can't be delegated.

Similarly, showing property to a buyer is an unleverageable service. The result is that realtor production quickly plateaus because much of the time required to run the business can't be scaled. Sure, they can get an assistant to process closing documents and solve problems, but there's a limit to scalability when the business is a personal service. Dentists, doctors and lawyers face the same challenge. Ultimately, they can hire out a lot of the process and services around their time, but at the end of the day, they are still the experts providing the core service and there is only so much work they can do.

IN SUMMARY

Systems are the way you, as the business owner, can empower others to run large parts of your business as if you were doing it personally.

Systems are freedom, and the structured rules that support your systems are freedom. Many people get confused and view structure as confining in a way that limits creativity, but the opposite is true. Structure defines the rules of how things work, which then allows you to create around those rules. The structure provides the framework within which creativity happens.

Using music as an example, the rules of melody and harmony convert noise into beautiful music. Similarly, your systems define the rules that govern your actions so mundane daily habits harmonize into a desirable outcome. These constructs remove most of the decision making so you can focus your limited bandwidth on the few creative tasks and important decisions that really matter.

Systems serve to open up creativity and bring freedom. If you want to own your business (rather than letting it own you) you need to remove yourself from the production process. Make it "system dependent," not "individual dependent." Make technology systems and standard operating procedures produce the results; not specific people.

It can take time and effort to get systems leverage working for you, but it's time well spent because the result is greater wealth, less risk, and more freedom. And that's a goal well worth pursuing.

EXERCISE: MAKE YOURSELF UNNECESSARY

The objective of this exercise is to isolate those activities that you, and only you, should be doing.

Everything else should be leveraged away. You want to take "you" out of the production equation because when you're the cog, you become the clog. You become the constraint to growth.

The process is simple. Look at every single thing that crosses your desk and assume that it's *a failure of your business systems*, simply by the fact that it found its way to your desk.

What standard operating procedure can you put in place so that the same issue doesn't cross your desk again?

How can it be delegated?

What technology system could manage it better than you?

If you treat every activity in your daily business life as a failure of the system and develop ways to leverage away all those tasks, pretty soon you'll be left with only those tasks that you alone should be working on. Those are the only tasks where leverage won't make good business sense.

This will increase the scalability of your business and increase your time freedom as well.

4 – COMMUNICATIONS AND MARKETING LEVERAGE

THE SHORTEST AND BEST WAY TO MAKE YOUR FORTUNE
IS TO LET PEOPLE SEE CLEARLY THAT IT IS
IN THEIR BEST INTEREST TO PROMOTE YOURS.

– JEAN DE LA BRUYERE

The 1954 Masters purse was $5,000. Fast forward to 2003 and it was 200 times larger at $1.08 million.

The average NBA salary was $8,000 in 1954. By 2003 it had climbed to $4.5 million.

In 1954, the average NFL player earned $16,000, but by 2003 the average player made $1.1 million.

What drove the dramatic increases in sports celebrity income?

If you answered "inflation" you'd be wrong. Surprisingly, it played a relatively small role compared to the real cause.

The main reason for the astonishing growth in sports celebrity earnings was communications leverage.

And the big change that caused huge growth in communications leverage between 1954 and 2003 was television entering the mass consumer market. Television made professional sports accessible to millions around the globe; whereas before television, viewership was limited to just a few thousand local fans.

Communications leverage expanded the audience size, making the product of sports entertainment more valuable. The result was increased advertising revenue, which translated into higher salaries for those sports celebrities who could attract the most eyeballs.

Without media, how would those athletes make those huge sums of money? Who would pay them? Communications leverage is what converted sports icons into millionaires.

Now let's contrast sports stars with teachers…

A teacher creates more value for society than a sports star; and yet, who commands the higher salary? Teachers' salaries remain low because they lack communications leverage. Today they teach to a roomful of pupils just as they did in 1954, so the salary they command has grown little net of inflation.

If teachers want to increase their income, they need to increase their leverage. They could get on the lecture circuit, attract media attention to their ideas, write books, produce educational videos for the mass market, develop a content marketing website around their ideas, and promote related educational products.

The point of these two examples is to illustrate how **communications leverage is the bridge that creates marketing value out of networks.** Stated another way, marketers use communications leverage with networks to grow their business and multiply income. In this chapter, I'll show you how each part of this formula works together in your wealth plan so you can get paid like a sports celebrity.

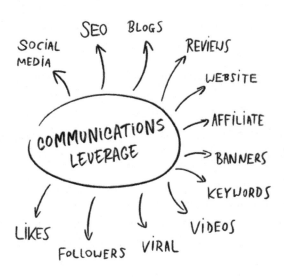

WHY COMMUNICATIONS LEVERAGE MATTERS

Communications leverage affects every business and impacts your daily life as a consumer.

Anytime you feel harried with information overload, look no further than the increased reach and reduced costs of communication technology. What started as stamps, a telegraph, and a telegram, was replaced by telephones, telex, fax, and conference calls, which then morphed into smart phones, the internet, videoconferencing, YouTube, podcasting, email, and instant messaging.

Each stage of this process increased access and lowered costs to communicate information. The result is tremendous communications leverage for your business, but information overload for consumers.

We're already seeing limits to how much information humans can effectively process without devolving into distraction. The instantaneous response expectations of today's zero latency, always-turned-on communications tools have introduced a new level of worker stress.

In fact, some research shows we've already exceeded the point of diminishing marginal returns on communications leverage – at least in terms of quality of life, if not business efficiency as well. Today's always-connected, over-communicated worker is maxed out, constantly distracted, and (often) burned out.

That doesn't mean you shouldn't use communications leverage in your business. It just means you'll want to carefully choose only those tools that deliver the highest leverage for your time while producing the least damaging side effects.

INCREASE YOUR PROFITS WITH MARKETING LEVERAGE

It's hard to get your message noticed. People have shorter attention spans, there's more information in front of your customer all the time, and your message is just one of millions that is trying to get through. You have to figure out how to cut through the noise with something meaningful or it will be too costly to connect with your target market.

There are several proven ways to increase the leverage in your marketing:

- Cross-sell, upsell, and back-end sell related products to existing clients for minimal additional marketing cost.

- Build systems to encourage your current clients to refer new clients.

- Joint-venture with non-competing businesses that share your same target market so you can promote your product or service to their client base, and vice versa.

- Nurture your sales funnel by delivering high-value information using technology systems previously discussed in the chapter on Systems Leverage.

- Create continuity sales programs, similar to a monthly membership program like iTunes or Netflix, so you earn recurring revenue from each sale.

- Advertise or write articles for publications that share the same target market, and include a great call to action at the bottom to encourage their readers to become your readers or even sign on for your services.

- Promote through a directory or list rental service that focuses on your target market.

In other words, there are many individual tactics to increase marketing leverage, but the good news is they can all be simplified into two strategic principles for application: find new customers and increase the lifetime value of your existing customers.

In fact, all marketing and communications leverage strategies for business boil down to just those two goals.

GOAL #1: INCREASE THE LIFETIME VALUE OF YOUR EXISTING CUSTOMERS

This is the starting point for marketing leverage because the easiest sale is a satisfied client who has already bought from you.

Research shows it takes seven calls to close a new client versus three calls to close an existing customer for the same product. Other research shows it's 10 times more expensive to land a new account than to serve an existing account.

That's because when a customer already knows, likes, and trusts you, and they're paying attention to your messaging, they're way more likely to buy from you. In fact, the only barrier between you and the next sale is having a great product that genuinely solves an important problem. Affinity, trust, and attention are already there for existing customers, which is why the sale is so much easier.

CROSS-SELL, UPSELL, AND BACK-END SELL

Do you like your cell phone carrier?

Almost nobody likes the company that provides their cell phone services. And that's largely because they are like so many businesses – dedicating their scarce resources to chasing new clients instead of first doing everything they can to better serve their existing clients.

In fact, it's far more effective to leverage your marketing by going *deeper* into your niche and developing a complete product line so you can cross-sell, upsell, and back-end sell to better serve your target clients.

Using Financial Mentor as an example, all of my courses backend each other. (https://financialmentor.com/educational-products/courses) Each is a targeted solution to a specific problem when one is pursuing financial independence, and all of the courses together provide a complete solution. The way it works in practice is that the customer enters the course series based on the problem immediately in front of them, and as soon as they solve that one problem, they are then confronted by the next naturally occurring problem in the wealth building process. The courses are arranged in the order that the problems naturally occur when one is in pursuit of financial freedom, so that one solution leads to the next, then the next, and so on until the goal is achieved.

Similarly, all of my books serve the same target market – people interested in financial independence. The entire product line serves a single market so that one sale on either platform can get leveraged into many sales across platforms.

For example, let's assume my Expectancy Wealth Planning course attracts 1000 customers and 100 affiliates. When I publish the next course in the series, that means I already have 1000 likely buyers, plus 100 affiliates to offer the course to for instant sales.

Not only that; the effect is multiplicative since every person who becomes interested in my teachings through the Expectancy Investing course is also a likely candidate for the Expectancy Wealth Planning course, as well as every other course and book in my product line. Each product backends every other product, thus increasing the lifetime value of every satisfied client.

The same thing happens at Amazon as a distributor of

my books. A cursory look at the "also bought" list for any of my books shows that people who buy one of my books tend to buy the rest of them. Each book holds a different marketing position by topic within Amazon (investing, retirement planning, financial coaching, variable annuities, leverage, risk management, etc.), which creates multiple ways for my target market to find my business when shopping on Amazon, and if they have a great reading experience, they then buy the other books. That's why the best way to expand my book business is to cross-sell by writing more books on different (but related) topics teaching how to achieve financial freedom.

Another way to increase the value of each customer is to repackage and repurpose existing products. For example, if you give a live seminar and record the presentation, you can sell it later as a DVD set. Or you can develop a live training, and then flesh it out later into a book or self-paced course. Or possibly you can take sections of a complete course and repackage them as books. In fact, the book you're reading right now is a stand-alone sampling of the three-lesson series fully explaining leverage, and it is excerpted from the entire Expectancy Wealth Planning course. If you're getting great value from this book, you'll get even more value from the comprehensive course it's excerpted from.

People prefer different modes of learning. Some like live events; others prefer books; and others want audio or video. Some people will consume everything in all formats! When you repurpose your products into multiple learning formats, it leverages your existing marketing efforts so you can sell more stuff to the same customers.

Also, when you train employees to always be on the lookout for an appropriate upsell or cross-sell for your related products, it increases the lifetime value of your customers. That's why the best servers ask if you'd like to have a drink or appetizer before your meal and also offer dessert before bringing the check. They'll also suggest great side dishes or add-ons to your meal. It improves your overall experience because you're well served, and it increases the profit margin of the business. These are high margin upsells for existing restaurant customers that significantly raise the average value of each client to the business.

CREATE CONTINUITY SALES PROGRAMS

The final strategy for increasing the lifetime value of your customers is continuity sales. The idea is simple: sell the customer on a repeat purchase program so they buy from you every month (rather than just one time), thus increasing the value of that sale. For example, don't just sell a single bottle of water. Instead, sell a weekly bottled water delivery service so that multiple bottles are sold every week.

In summary, when you fully satisfy your customers' needs through a complete product line, it gives them the opportunity to buy more from you, resulting in a higher lifetime value for each customer. It's one of the smartest ways to grow your business because it leverages the value of every dollar you spend on marketing to increase total sales.

GOAL #2: FIND NEW CUSTOMERS

There's a limit to how much of your stuff each customer needs. That's why finding new customers is the second goal of marketing leverage. And one of the most effective tools for reaching new customers is technology.

Technology is so deeply intertwined in all communications today – whether it's the phone, internet, email, or social media – that it's nearly impossible to talk about communications leverage in marketing without including *technology* leverage.

TECHNOLOGY FOR NURTURING YOUR SALES FUNNEL

Never in the history of business have more powerful marketing tools been available for so little cost, and this is because of technology. For example, a website provides the unique ability to track and segment both traffic and subscribers according to interest, and the cost to identify and reach out to specific target markets has never been cheaper. It's a marketer's goldmine of information:

- Use content marketing on the internet to attract people with interests that align with your product or service by delivering valuable information that builds trust and authority for your brand.

- Electronic mail systems can deliver valuable information to prospects at minimal cost so you can nurture new relationships into front-of-mind awareness for your brand or service.

- Electronic mail systems can also monitor and rank subscriber interest according to what they view on your website, so you only market to people likely to buy.

- A scheduling system can connect your email system to automate your entire sales funnel.

Leveraging technology in marketing has three important benefits:

1. Low marginal cost for each touch point. Technology is generally priced as a fixed expense, allowing you to cost-effectively increase the frequency and breadth of communication.

2. Building brand loyalty and trust by giving value through courses, videos, and other educational resources that solve your target customer's problems. Technology is what allows you to communicate all that value cost effectively.

3. Immediate data proving effectiveness. In the old days of snail-mail, marketers would pay large upfront costs to design, print, and mail a campaign. Or they'd incur large media advertising

costs. Then they'd have to wait weeks to monitor the results and find out if their marketing idea was effective. Today, you can test a headline in Google or test-email an offer to part of your list for just pennies and know within minutes how effective it was.

The value of generating immediate response data can't be overstated. You no longer have to risk thousands up front and wait weeks to gauge success or failure. Instead, you can test an offer for almost no cost and know the conversion rate within minutes.

You can also tweak the offer based on your test results, and then send it to another sample portion of your list. This shortens the marketing learning curve through rapid iteration, which streamlines the efficiency of all marketing with minimal waste.

HOW MARKETING AND NETWORKING WORK HAND-IN-HAND

Another group of leveraged marketing tactics you can use to reach new customers interconnects with network leverage.

The four most common forms of network leverage applied to marketing are:

1.   Media and publicity

2. Bulk sales

3. Joint ventures

4. Referral systems

When you land a spot on TV or receive newspaper coverage, you leverage the publication's subscriber base. You produce content once and your message reaches thousands. Another advantage of media marketing is that the message enters the prospect's mind through an unlocked back door. It's perceived as unbiased information reporting vetted by a trusted third party...instead of self-promotion copy. Examples of leveraging media include:

- Publishing a case study to a specific industry showing how you excelled at helping one of their own. This allows others in that industry who want the same help to seek you out. You promote the story by telling industry publications what you did, provide data to support your claims, and then deliver on the interviews.

- Be a guest on relevant podcasts for interviews. It positions you as the trusted expert because you're the invited guest of a host who has an existing trust relationship with the listeners. Interviews are usually 30 to 60 minutes long and can be delivered in audio or video format over the internet. The intimate format and implied authority as an expert guest builds extraordinary relationship with the audience as you discuss topics relevant to your subject matter expertise.

- Promoting the awards your business receives. For example, Financial Mentor has received numerous awards, including "Best Retirement Planning Site," "Best Designed Website," and "People's Choice," and the news of these awards has in turn been picked up by major media outlets and republished. These awards are valuable because they're a third-party endorsement of your business, adding credibility while also reaching new clients.

Each media strategy alone is powerful, but combining several of these marketing leverage techniques can dramatically increase the authority and trustworthiness of your business.

Another marketing strategy that includes network leverage is to bulk sell to strategic partners. For example, Microsoft was built from Bill Gates negotiating a single bulk licensing agreement with IBM that sold millions of copies of software, making Microsoft the industry standard for computer operating systems worldwide. Millions of sales all stemmed from just one sale by leveraging IBM's sales network.

A slight twist on the same theme is joint ventures, where you offer your product to someone else's customers on a split revenue agreement. The affiliate leverages your product by profiting from something he didn't create, and you leverage the affiliate's customer base and opt-in list so you can sell inside a trusted network you otherwise couldn't access.

You can also leverage other people's networks when you hire commission-only sales people. It's essentially risk-free sales to your business because you only pay for the results the salesperson produces from marketing to his network.

IN SUMMARY

There are two objectives you're trying to achieve with marketing leverage. You want to:

- Increase the lifetime value of every customer
- Reach more people to grow your customer base.

The acceleration of communications leverage through improvements in technology has changed how modern marketers achieve these two goals by lowering the cost to share information so you can affordably increase both reach and frequency in your marketing.

However, the same technology that's leveraged to increase marketing communications has simultaneously brought information overwhelm to your target market. People are distracted, harried, and have less bandwidth than ever to pay attention to your message.

This makes it harder than ever to break through the

information clutter so you can connect with your target market and grow your business.

Stated another way, you must use communications leverage tools in your marketing to compete effectively, but you have to be really smart about how you apply these tools so you deliver value and serve people rather than just adding to all the noise already out there.

EXERCISE: INCREASE YOUR CUSTOMER LIFETIME VALUE

The goal of this exercise is for you to start thinking about ways you can increase the lifetime value of each customer in your business.

This principle can be applied to nearly every type of business. For example, you might be tempted to think upsells and cross-sells don't relate to your real estate rental business, but they absolutely do. Two obvious strategies are renting laundry equipment to your tenant or offering coin-operated vending. Your tenants need clean laundry. By providing them with equipment they pay for, you meet their need and increase their lifetime value to your real estate rental business.

CPA's historically traded time for money providing accounting and tax preparation services…until recent years. It was a natural upsell for that profession to offer investment and insurance products because they were already intimately familiar with the client's financial numbers and had an established, trusted relationship with the client as a financial expert.

The same principle is being applied when you open an investment brokerage account and then weeks later they start mailing you credit card offers attached to your account as an upsell.

Regardless of your business, these principles can be applied to better serve your clients by profitably solving their problems. Below are several questions to help you find potential ideas:

- What new products and services could you create that would solve an important problem for your clients so that you could upsell or cross-sell?

- What products are offered by your competitors that would be perfect for your customers and that you'd be happy to promote for an affiliate commission?

- How could you convert a one-time sale into a continuity sale?

- What continuity programs are your customers already consuming that you could adapt to your business?

5 – NETWORK AND RELATIONSHIP LEVERAGE

SOMEDAY THIS WILL BE TRUE FOR ALL OF US:
OUR NETWORK WILL EQUAL OUR NET WORTH.

– TIM SANDERS

NETWORKS EXCHANGE VALUE, NOT MONEY

Imagine you want to travel from Los Angeles to New York.

You don't need to own the highway or an airline. You don't need to own a car, rent a car, pay for gas, or even buy an airline ticket.

All you need to do is find someone who wants a car delivered from L.A. to New York or has shipping needs that require an airline ticket for the baggage that you could accompany on the plane. You could provide the delivery service and accomplish your travel goal at the same time without paying a dime.

In other words, the only thing standing between you and the trip you desire is not money, cars, airline tickets, or gas. You don't need any of those resources. You just need the network and relationships to connect your goal with someone else's.

Network and relationship leverage is about shifting your mindset from buying and renting resources to the purposeful cultivation of ***relationships that exchange value***.

That's a key point so I'll repeat it – network leverage is based on relationships that exchange value instead of money. It might be contacts, resources, strategies, experiences, referrals, support, or any other form of value that costs the giver nothing but makes a big difference for the receiver. Giving value is how both parties support each other.

It's an effective leverage tool because at the root of all business is a human relationship. No aspect of business exists outside of relationship, whether it's customer, supplier, employee, partner, shareholder, contractor, or professional adviser relationships.

All business is human relationship. When you know how to leverage those relationships ethically, you'll create more business, faster, and with less of your own resources.

YOUR MOST VALUABLE ASSET

Your success is dramatically impacted by the people you know.

Each addition to your network gives you more resources,

experience, and support to draw from. Strong relationships can deliver talents, skills, contacts, and credibility you might otherwise not be able to access.

- People in your network can provide insights and share solutions based on their own experience.

- They can help you realize you're not alone because they've faced professional challenges similar to your own.

- They can provide options for partnerships, new customers, and information useful to your business.

- They can encourage and support you.

- They can hold you accountable to overcome challenges and make the most of professional opportunities.

- They can open doors that would otherwise be closed.

For example, Financial Mentor is a financial education business built around content marketing on the internet. This is a rapidly developing new field akin to the Wild, Wild West where every operator is literally creating their own rules on the fly because the business develops and changes so rapidly.

I operated as a lone wolf for years until the Financial Bloggers' Conference was created by Philip Taylor. This conference connects 100's of financial bloggers with varying levels of expertise and specialized niches in a community built around sharing best practices for what is working today. I attend every year, and I learn so much from my network of peers that I have to reformulate my business plans after every conference.

The key point is: network leverage is much more than just a Rolodex of names and contact details. It's a carefully chosen group of peers that you interact with, or want to begin interacting with, on a regular basis.

The key is not just to build a large network, because size alone isn't sufficient to deliver value. Instead, you want to carefully choose and nurture your network because several factors determine the value of that network:

- **Size** – The larger your network, the more valuable it becomes.

- **Quality** – Do they understand your needs? What resources can they access?

- **Depth** – Long-term relationships deepened over years have the greatest value.

- **Recency** – You must regularly contribute to the relationship or it will degrade over time.

- **Relevancy** – Is their expertise related to what you do?

BUT I DON'T WANT TO "USE" MY FRIENDS

Unfortunately, despite the huge potential value of network leverage, many people remain uncomfortable with the whole idea.

- It might feel disingenuous, like you're analyzing relationships based on their resources and usefulness, rather than based on friendship alone.

- Or it might feel dangerously close to exploiting your friends for profit.

- Some people feel it's insincere or manipulative—an elegant way of using people.

- Task-oriented workers may feel that connecting with people is little more than a distraction from their "real work" of getting the job done.

All of these criticisms are valid, but only if you approach network leverage the wrong way.

There's a sincere, non-exploiting, highly productive way to build your network based on *giving first* that feels natural and appropriate to both parties.

Let's look at how network leverage is done right so everyone can feel *great* about the business relationships they build.

4 STEPS TO BUILD A NETWORK THAT MULTIPLIES YOUR WEALTH

STEP 1: DECIDE WHO YOU WANT IN YOUR NETWORK

The starting point is to decide who you want in your network.

That requires you to first look inward at what you're trying to accomplish, before looking outward at who can help you accomplish it. Your own personal long-term goals need to connect with the goals for your network strategy. That means having an understanding of the purpose of your networking – and who you need to meet and build relationships with in the long term to reach your goals.

For example, when I began attending the FinCon conference referenced earlier, my goal was to connect with financial bloggers who were more successful or more advanced in the business than myself. Back then, it was like the Wild, Wild West because there was no proven business model. It was all new, so everyone was making it up as they went along. One person had mastered advertising; another, affiliate marketing; another, search engine optimization; and another, audience engagement; but nobody had mastered all the components of the business. Each blogger had something to share, bringing different experience to the table, but we were all in essentially the same business. The result is we've all grown our businesses faster and with fewer mistakes by sharing our knowledge.

The key is to have clearly defined targets; otherwise you might build an extensive network, but it might not be relevant to what you need.

- You could choose to develop your network around professional interests like engineering, product development, marketing, sales and the like.

- It could be based on a business model – for example, internet marketer, or manufacturing with a typical supply chain, or B to B, or B to C.

- Or it could be based on filling gaps in your plan where it's particularly weak.

Once you decide the types of people you'd like to have in your network, the next step is to target specific people instead of targeting a whole company. Go narrow and deep (versus wide and broad).

- Find out who makes the relevant decisions at the companies you are targeting. You can usually find this information by checking corporate press releases, LinkedIn, and the speaker roster (and topics) from industry events.

- What are the various high leverage relationships you can develop? Professional, collegial, mastermind, and client relationships all offer tremendous upside potential.

STEP 2: CONNECT WITH THOSE PEOPLE

Now that you have your targeted list of contacts, the next step is to communicate with them.

Every relevant relationship is an opportunity to ask questions, solve problems, share resources, and strategize to expand your knowledge base. Be a good listener. Learn from every interaction.

Go where the right people go so you can meet them. If you need funding, network with funders. If you need to learn something, network with people who know the answers. If you want to sell, network with potential buyers. Always be developing relationships with people who are one step ahead of where you're taking your business in the future. That way, when the need arises, you can pick up the phone and make it happen.

Starting the relationship need not be any more complicated than creating a conversation. Be interesting and interested by asking relevant questions that further the conversation, rather than giving answers that end it.

Smart, thoughtful questions further the conversation and deepen the relationship by getting people talking about themselves. Most people won't just open up naturally, but if prompted in an engaging way, they'll tell you more than you ever thought you needed to know. The key is you have to be genuinely interested.

Meeting people to initially break the ice has never been

easier than with the internet. Social media puts you within reach of nearly every person, regardless of celebrity status, as long as you're willing to make an effort to cultivate the relationship.

Because of social media, you should never cold-call or cold-email anymore. With LinkedIn and Twitter you can break the ice in an innocuous, comfortable way.

Discussion forums and LinkedIn groups can provide a lot of information and feedback. You can send out a question and get multiple expert replies. Sometimes an entire discussion will erupt online, fleshing out all the intricacies of your question.

Don't underestimate the value of weak ties made online. The "6 degrees of separation" principle that connects all of us gets smaller all the time. There's huge combined wisdom, connections, and opportunities in your network – even at the casual level.

Online connections may not be as strong as in-person relationships, but they can still provide valuable feedback and referrals that eventually lead to in-person and telephone relationships. As you follow up with your online connections, you'll build those relationships into something deeper and more valuable for both parties.

The way you efficiently nurture your weak ties into stronger relationships is through scalable communication strategies. A weekly blog post, email list, and regular social media updates will help you maintain consistent contact with your entire network and can expand your network to include new people you've never met. Use this scalable update strategy to help people en masse while also reminding people of what you do.

Forming a mastermind group is another way to apply network leverage where each member of the group benefits from the knowledge, experience, and network of every other member because of the trust relationship that's built through the ongoing mastermind format.

Another way to find connections relevant to your business is through resources such as the SBA's SCORE and its classes, and through government agency programs, foundations, or corporations with similar interests.

Participate in professional associations. For example, an attorney might help out with his local bar association, or a female executive could join the National Association of Female Executives (NAFE) and the National Association of Women Business Owners (NAWBO).

Finally, you could take the traditional approach of simply meeting other professionals for coffee or lunch on a regular basis.

In short, there are many ways to initially meet the people with whom you'd like to build your network. Just pick the strategy you're most comfortable with and get started.

STEP 3: BUILD THE RELATIONSHIP

Once you've opened the door with that first contact, the key to building a genuine relationship is to focus on the other person's needs, not your own. Pay it forward. Your first concern should be: "What's in it for them?"

Staying with the example of the FinCon conference, it's the most valuable and enjoyable business event I've ever attended because the entire culture is rooted in giving first. That's because the attendees were writers in the business of helping their audience with their finances. The very nature of the business model was to first give your best knowledge generously, and then it comes back through other channels. This resulted in a conference of givers sharing their best business advice, simply because that's their habitual business behavior. It's what makes the conference so valuable.

The way to connect during conversations is to be interested and interesting. When you meet someone with common interests, follow up promptly with an email to establish that common connection for relationship. Stay fresh in their minds by reaching out every one or two months to share something of interest that's valuable – a resource or news item related to their needs.

Actively listen to the other person to find out their needs because you're genuinely interested in being helpful. Always seek to add more value than you take away. You care about the other person and their challenges, and you're willing to give value where appropriate.

Be the first to offer up your contacts and resources before you make demands on the relationship. Recognize that the rule of reciprocity is implied in human relationships. It's never overtly required, but research has shown that most people feel it nonetheless. So give generously and don't worry about what comes back.

Your giving doesn't have to be anything big. Just a small gesture at the right moment can open doors for the other person and build value. Some ideas include:

- Providing an unsolicited introduction to some-body in the same industry.

- Sending a link to an interesting article related to what they're working on.

- Or it could be as simple as a supportive fol-low-up call regarding a challenge they were facing.

Just remember to keep all communications succinct because everyone is busy. Always think about how you can provide value, respond quickly, and keep the con-versation going while respecting the other person's time.

STEP 4: HOW TO ASK FOR HELP

Eventually you build the relationship to a point where it's appropriate to ask for help. After all, a highly valuable network is only useful if you use it.

Fortunately, this is never a problem when you build it right, because the context of well-developed relationship removes any discomfort in asking because your intent has been genuine from the beginning – so the other person wants to help you just as you would want to help them.

There are very few business problems that your peers haven't already experienced in their career. So they can empathize with your situation and are happy to help by sharing their experience – whether by arranging introductions or offering advice. Someone always knows someone who can give you exactly what you need – whether a restaurant recommendation or an introduction to a key decision maker for the deal of your lifetime. But if you don't ask, you won't get it.

When asking, be clear and concise with your request and expectations because everyone is busy. Connect whatever you're asking for help with to previous conversations, so it doesn't come out of left field.

For example, a simple ask could be something like: *"Per our previous conversation about the financing challenges I'm facing, I've decided to start looking for angel investors interested in app development projects. I was hoping you could provide a quick intro to that investor you worked with in Portland last summer."*

Notice how the ask is completely related to previous discussions so there is nothing awkward in the request. It's just a logical next step in an ongoing communication between the two of you.

NETWORK AND RELATIONSHIP LEVERAGE IN PRACTICE

If you are still feeling uncomfortable or don't quite see how this sort of leverage works, I understand. The best way to go about building these sorts of networks is to commit your time and energy to groups and missions where you share a personal interest. You must be genuinely interested in the networks in which you are investing your time and energy. For example:

- Volunteer or organize volunteers for a community program you believe in.

- Enroll your community in your cause.

    - For example, my kid's school enrolls parents to donate their time in the classrooms, for fundraisers, and for community events to support their children's education.

- Join (or create) a mastermind group. Leverage and add to the knowledge, experience, contacts and resources of others, plus gain accountability.

- Attend classes and programs that interest you. Meet and mix with the attendees and presenters.

- Teach a program that adds value to your audience and make yourself the hub of that community.

Whatever way you choose to build your network and relationships, make sure that you are adding as much value as you are receiving. That is the key to building genuine connections.

You can find more network leverage ideas in "101+ Leverage Hacks: A Cheat Sheet for Quickly Implementing Leverage in Your Wealth Plan" at https://financialmentor.com/free-stuff/leverage-book.

LEVERAGING YOUR CUSTOMER NETWORK

Don't just limit yourself to professional or peer networking! Your customer network can be an excellent source of referrals and connections as well.

Referrals from your client network are the next best thing to an existing customer because there's implicit trust in the referred relationship.

Your goal as a businessperson is to provide such a great product or service that customers will enthusiastically "thank you" for all the value they have received. When that happens, you need to have a mechanism built right into your business system that invites a referral. After all, nobody wants to ask their clients intrusive questions like "Who can you recommend me to?" or "Do you know anybody that could use my product?"

Instead, you want to build referral systems that encourage your clients to spread the word about your great products.

- The required first step for customer referrals is developing a truly remarkable product or service that is worth referring to others. Referral systems only work when people feel that they're *helping* their friends or business associates with their referral. "Remarkable" could be as simple as being a contractor who returns calls, delivers on time, and completes the job under bid (since that's so rare), or it could be a product that solves a key problem. The point is: it must "wow" existing clients because nobody refers a product or service unless it stands out.

- Second, you have to design a process that refers others as a natural part of how you do business – so you never have to ask those intrusive questions. It could be a financial incentive or a bonus for referrals; or it could be structured into the original agreement as a condition for completion so that it's fully expected; or it could be as simple as sharing a link to the sales page.

Finally, you'll want to set up a follow-up system to prompt making the referrals and also communicate what resulted from the referrals to complete the communication loop. And *always* thank the referrer for their support! Referring a friend or colleague is the ultimate compliment, so acknowledge each referral with an appropriate "thank you."

When someone gives you a referral, it's important to follow up in a relatively short period of time. If the individual has called his contact and given that person your name, you want to follow up while your name is still fresh in that person's mind.

It is also a good idea to let the original contact know what is happening with the referral. Send an e-mail to the referral and copy the referral source. That way, the referral source is reminded that you are out there; the referral source sees that you are a person of *action*; and the referral is reminded of your connection to the referral source. You can also send a letter to the referral source updating him or her. Then if the referral leads to anything, let the original contact know about it and thank the contact again.

IN SUMMARY

The key point of this chapter is that no business exists within a vacuum; all business is done through relationship, which is why relationship leverage is so valuable.

Building a network is worth the effort because strategic alliances with the right people can either make or break your wealth plan. The value of a solid piece of advice at just the right time, or getting the chance to work with someone who has deep experience in your industry, can be game-changing.

Be creative and opportunistic in how you meet people, and build the relationship by focusing your efforts on giving and paying it forward. Play the long game.

Building a strong professional network of strategic contacts is something that can take years. Like investing for retirement or college, what you get out in the end has a lot to do with what you put into it. It takes effort, but the compound return on that effort can make or break your results.

Furthermore, the sooner you start investing in your network, the larger the rewards are down the road. But before you start making withdrawals, make sure you have built a strong "nest egg" of good will. If you allow your business relationships to grow over time, your contacts will be much more helpful to you when you do finally start asking for advice.

With the right relationships you can accomplish nearly anything. The key is who you know, what you know, and how you ethically apply those resources.

EXERCISE: BUILD YOUR NETWORK

Identify one person who's already built a business similar to what you want to create. The similarity might be in terms of revenue model, size, industry vertical, or choice of technology.

Reach out to that person.

This could be a simple email and possibly follow-up phone calls. Or maybe you "stalk" him a bit on Twitter or in blog comments before taking it further.

Build the relationship by asking smart questions, providing genuine acknowledgments, taking his advice when provided, and following up with your results.

Sometimes it can be as simple as paying for 20 minutes of the person's time on an advice website like Clarity.FM – if they're high profile or a media personality; but most of the time it will take much more effort.

The point is to network up and build connections that can take you to the next level of growth.

Once you've completed this assignment for one person, then rinse and repeat by creating a list of people who can help you achieve your goal.

Then reach out to them and build genuine connections.

6 – KNOWLEDGE AND EXPERIENCE LEVERAGE

KNOWLEDGE IS OF TWO KINDS.
WE KNOW A SUBJECT OURSELVES, OR WE KNOW
WHERE WE CAN FIND INFORMATION UPON IT.

– SAMUEL JOHNSON

Knowledge is the foundation of all wealth-generating processes.

Without knowledge, natural resources would just be dormant in the ground. Knowledge is what converts resources into something with economic value.

Similarly, most of the value of manufactured goods is in the knowledge behind the manufacturing processes that create them.

In other words, physical capital owes most of its value to intellectual capital, but the connection ends there because physical and intellectual capital each have very different characteristics.

Intellectual capital is different because it's created out of thin air, retained, and distributed without any limits. It's limitless because it's an infinite resource (unlike land, buildings, machinery). Physical capital is limited to the resources in your possession.

In addition, intellectual capital is different from physical capital because each time you transfer knowledge the recipient is enriched, but nothing physically leaves the creator. Both can possess the same knowledge, thus creating greater abundance. Physical capital is different because it leaves you when you give it away, making you poorer. Only one person can possess it, thus creating scarcity.

Intellectual capital grows when used and depreciates when not used. Physical capital does the opposite because it gets consumed through use and depreciates in value.

Intellectual Capital	Physical Capital
Knowledge (including know-how, skills and expertise)	Money (including physical items you can purchase with it)
Relationships	Land
Company Secrets	Buildings
Databases	Machinery
Networks	Goods
Processes and Systems	Natural Resources

These differences are important to growing your business. Knowledge shared between two people effectively doubles the amount of knowledge capital within your business, and there's no price to pay for that growth. That makes knowledge leverage a key tool in your wealth building arsenal.

But surprisingly, it's an asset that's rarely valued properly, thus opening up opportunity for competitive advantage.

One of the reasons many people misunderstand knowledge as an asset is because physical capital's inherent limitations have conditioned us to think in terms of scarcity, but knowledge is different because you can give it freely and it can still give back to you. It operates under a different set of economics.

For example, the more I give away my knowledge freely on the Financial Mentor website (https://financial mentor.com), the more the business grows. The key is to find cost-efficient forms of communication that create more value to the business than they cost. Email newsletters, video, and podcasts are all examples.

The Grateful Dead are often credited with being early pioneers in this strategy. They were known for their live shows and they allowed a massive bootleg market of live show recordings to develop, for which they received no compensation. It was all freely distributed music. This created a loyal fan base who also bought their studio albums and ensured that all their live shows throughout the world would sell out immediately with no advertising or promotion.

In short, the intellectual capital of free bootleg recordings did all the promotion without them spending a dime, and this strategy foreshadowed similar content marketing strategies on the internet three decades later.

THE 2 TYPES OF KNOWLEDGE CAPITAL

Leveraging intellectual capital is important because the essence of business competition is relentless innovation to develop a competitive advantage. The source of that innovation is knowledge.

The idea is to always work smarter, not harder. You hire people smarter than yourself and innovate for greater efficiency. You don't have to reinvent the wheel to improve. Everything you need to know already exists if you can just find the correct source of knowledge to leverage.

But before we can leverage knowledge, it's helpful to organize it in two different ways:

- **Tacit or Unrecorded** – knowledge that only exists in someone's head, making it hard to leverage through sharing.

- **Explicit or Recorded** – knowledge that has been documented in some way so it's easy to share and leverage.

Notice how knowledge and systems leverage connect. A system is where you convert tacit knowledge into explicit knowledge through a business system.

Examples of recorded knowledge as part of a business system include...

- Bootleg recordings of Grateful Dead shows
- A book

- An online article
- Courses
- Videos
- A standard operating procedure

Each of these examples is a form of explicit or recorded knowledge leverage creating intellectual capital. The key point is that *when tacit knowledge is made explicit through documentation or recording, it lowers the cost of distribution.*

That's why knowledge leverage is also connected to technology leverage because technology has created an unprecedented growth in cost efficient ways to make tacit knowledge explicit and then distribute that knowledge so it can compound. Similarly, information sharing is multiplied through network leverage using wireless communications, high speed internet, and multi-media communications.

As stated in earlier chapters, all of the leverage types are more connected than what appears on the surface, and this is yet another example of how that works.

Similarly, knowledge leverage is related to time leverage because you don't have enough time to do everything; so you surround yourself with a specialized team of advisors, coaches, mentors, employees, vendors – that deliver the expertise you lack so you can grow your wealth and achieve your financial goals.

KNOWLEDGE VERSUS INFORMATION

The problem with knowledge is that it's frequently confused with information. But knowledge is more closely aligned with *experience* because you can't truly know something until you have direct experience applying the information.

Knowledge requires the mental process of understanding, comprehension, and learning inside your mind. It results from absorbing information and applying it through action resulting in experience.

Conversely, the equation flips upside down when you want to communicate knowledge because the only alternative is to create messages of information. This information doesn't carry knowledge, but it can be assimilated, organized, and applied by the recipient into their own knowledge structures. The receiver's knowledge will be different from the transmitter's, even though it's the same information – because of the different experience base, values, and perceptions unique to the recipient that color that information and affect how it's assimilated.

Using this book as an example, I have direct knowledge through experience of the wealth building strategies that I communicate via the instruction in this book. You then reassemble that instruction into your own knowledge. The more you work with and repeat the learning, the more accurate your knowledge will become. But your knowledge and my knowledge will never be identical because our experience is different.

Same Information

+

Different Experience

=

Different Knowledge

It's a bit of an intellectual distinction, but it's a mistake commonly made and worth understanding because it connects to risk management, which is a central principle to strategically building wealth and investing for more consistent, profitable returns.

The greater your knowledge based on actual experience, the lower your risk.

For example, you can read information about mountain climbing and you can attend classes. But your risk of making a catastrophic mistake is dramatically higher than someone with 20 years of actual climbing experience.

Same information about climbing + less experience = increased risk of failure

Your risk of failure is always greatest when you have only information, but little direct experience. As your experience increases, information turns to knowledge and risk declines.

With that said, let's look at the three different ways you can leverage knowledge:

- Leveraging your time by hiring the expertise of others.
- Leveraging your own knowledge by becoming the go-to expert.
- Leveraging the knowledge already inside your organization.

HIRE THE EXPERT

Let's start with hiring an expert.

As stated earlier, hiring a team of people so you can benefit from the specialized expertise you lack is closely aligned with time leverage. You can't master the intricacies of everything, so the smart alternative is to hire experts that live and breathe a given subject every working day as their profession.

For example, maybe you want to explore rent-to-own real estate but you have questions. You could spend days researching the subject to try and gain the necessary expertise, fact checking and resolving all the contradictory information.

Or you could contact someone who lives and breathes

the subject every working day because that's his profession. Get someone who has spent years learning the intricacies of their craft and pay them for efficient access to that depth of knowledge, thus saving you time and headaches, and frequently money (if you find the right expert).

In this example, the expert can immediately advise you regarding how to do rent-to-own; warn you about the tricks and traps to watch out for; connect you to the best resources; include ready-to-go legal contracts; and provide you with everything you need to make it happen, all in a one-hour consultation.

The point is: you're not just leveraging the knowledge and experience that a true expert can deliver; you're also leveraging his contacts and resources to save you implementation time while also expanding your network.

It rarely makes sense to use your scarce time re-creating the wheel when someone else is better qualified and can do it faster and cheaper. Time that you spend learning about each profession so you can do-it-yourself is time you're not spending working on your business.

Instead, the smart alternative is to leverage the intelligence, time, and experience of others. Find people who have walked the path before you, learn from them, hire them, and model their behavior. They have the knowledge.

But this brings up an important distinction regarding

the complexity of the task and the frequency of use. For example, I hire experts for complex coding tasks and system development on my website because the complexity would take me way too much time and effort to master.

However, every week my work requires simple coding tasks that take less time and hassle to do myself than it would take to explain to someone else. The result is I've trained myself to do basic coding for simple tasks that occur regularly.

When it comes time to develop these new skills, one of my favorite strategies to save money is to buy an information *product* (where the knowledge is made explicit) rather than a service solution where the knowledge is tacit. For example, you could hire my personal coaching services to teach you how to use leverage to accelerate your wealth growth, but technology leverage has made this knowledge explicit through this book for pennies on the dollar. Similarly, I offer an entire course teaching you how to design your personalized wealth plan (that this book is excerpted from and that took over two years of full-time effort to build); and you can leverage all that knowledge for little more than it would cost to coach with me for an hour, all because of technology and marketing leverage.

Books and courses are two of my favorite cost-effective sources for explicit knowledge leverage, giving you access to experts you otherwise could never learn from. You can also access explicit knowledge from podcasts, educational audio sets, webinars, and other educational resources.

In summary, hiring an expert as a service makes good business sense when you need the expert's personal involvement. Leveraging their knowledge through a product makes sense when you just need the information.

BECOME THE EXPERT

The second way you can apply knowledge leverage is to master a subject so deeply that you become a high-demand expert in the field. This is an appropriate strategy when your goal is to increase your hourly earning capacity.

The key idea is: you become the expert who knows what others wished they knew, so they gladly pay to leverage your knowledge. It's the mirror image of the previous "hire the expert" strategy where you become the expert that others hire, increasing your income as a result.

Supply and demand dictates that money follows that which is in rare supply by forcing higher prices. There's no shortage of ignorance, but genuine expertise that solves high value problems is rare.

That means a proven path to increasing your income is to compound the growth of your intellectual capital first, and then sell that knowledge so others can leverage it.

The way you elevate yourself to expert status is by building a platform that showcases your expertise. Example strategies include:

- Write useful, cutting-edge articles.
- Pursue free publicity by being a guest expert on other experts' podcasts.
- Be interviewed by other writers for publication in other media outlets.
- Write a book. ☺

Expert positioning changes your service business from a commodity service provider competing based on price, to an in-demand, go-to expert that commands premium pricing. You immediately increase your time-for-money hourly earning capacity.

In investing, this concept is known as "an edge," and in business it's called "a competitive advantage." It's where your knowledge and experience built into your business offerings are so superior that there's really no competition.

Experts with specialized, high-value knowledge can negotiate deals based on performance (instead of hourly rate), allowing you to leverage the client's business for profit so that it's not dependent on your time.

For example, an online marketing expert or course development expert could hire herself out for a percentage of the income generated. She could create a single marketing funnel that could pay millions of dollars in the right situation, or she could earn long-term residual income based on a percentage of sales for a course she developed for a high-profile expert who lacked the back-end product and didn't have the time to create it any other way.

These agreements can be extremely lucrative if you're good, and if you can identify businesses with large gaps in profitability that you can remedy.

Alternatively, you can repackage your high-value knowledge into books, courses, video instruction, and other information products. Think of it as knowledge-in-a-box by converting your knowledge from tacit to explicit. This changes your expert business from service to product-based revenue so you can create a scalable business model that disconnects the relationship between time and money.

In short, when you establish yourself as a high-value expert, there are multiple ways to leverage that knowledge into dramatically increased income for your wealth plan.

DON'T FORGET THE KNOWLEDGE INSIDE YOUR ORGANIZATION

Finally, the third way to leverage knowledge is to better manage the knowledge already inside your organization.

No business can function without the knowledge inside the head of various staff members as well as the shared knowledge that makes up all the systems that govern how the business operates.

If you're not clear on the value of the intellectual capital inside your business, just imagine everyone in your company losing their memory so that all knowledge related to the business is now gone. Then arrive the next day at work with nobody knowing what to do and try operating the business to turn a profit. Nothing would work.

Now imagine how much it would cost you to recreate the lost intellectual capital and to restore all business operations to their former functionality; and that should give you some idea how valuable the knowledge is inside your organization.

Unfortunately, many businesses don't value knowledge as a resource that must be managed and leveraged, thus causing missed opportunities to improve business processes and to secure and improve profitability through the innovative ideas of staff. These businesses are also in danger of letting important knowledge walk out the door when employees leave.

Equally surprising is how some companies will hire consultants at exorbitant fees when they already have the required expertise just down the hall – at no additional cost.

One leverage strategy to better use the knowledge in your business is to multiply the intellectual capital through internal training processes, so that unique, proprietary knowledge about customers, competitors, products, and techniques that resides in the mind of one employee gets shared with many other employees. This is critical so that no single employee has sole possession of unique and important knowledge.

This connects back to technology leverage and standard operating procedures where employees commit their tacit knowledge into *explicit* knowledge through training materials that make it efficient to share, thus ensuring it never gets lost.

This requires creating both a culture and infrastructure within the organization that supports knowledge sharing and provides the resources to make it happen. *It won't happen on its own.* It must be dictated from the top and built right into how the business operates.

If the organization's climate is highly competitive, only junk will be shared. Employees will feel too insecure to share their best stuff because it would risk giving away their competitive advantage. Reward systems must be created to encourage sharing.

In short, the business needs to build an entire *process* to promote, nurture, and distribute knowledge among employees; one that addresses the following four requirements:

- **Gathering:** Locate new knowledge worth distributing – without cluttering the system with unnecessary information. This will require an expert within the company to be responsible for locating and filtering the available information.

- **Distribution:** Efficiently distribute the necessary knowledge *only* to the people who can use it, thus avoiding information overload. This might involve a company newsletter, or "lunch and learns," or possibly a curated library.

- **Implementation:** It's not enough to collect and distribute information. You must convert the shared information into usable systems and strategies that result in business growth.

- **Improvement:** Knowledge can become obsolete very quickly, so it always needs to be improved and updated. This necessitates a knowledge archive with someone responsible for continually identifying outdated, irrelevant information and ensuring that it's removed or updated.

Leverage the accumulated knowledge and experience contained both inside and outside your business to create a competitive advantage. This increases your income and accelerates your wealth plan so you can achieve financial freedom faster.

IN SUMMARY

Personal knowledge and learning are limited by the time you have available and your ability to comprehend and internalize information. Experience results from gathering the relevant information and then applying it to master your desired skills. Remember: all knowledge is limited by the amount of time you have to commit to gaining the necessary experience, because there's always more to learn than time to learn it. That's why hiring an expert who lives and breathes the knowledge you require can be such an effective leverage strategy to save you time and accelerate your wealth.

Alternatively, if your goal is to increase your hourly earning capacity, it might make sense to gather the knowledge yourself so as to become the go-to expert that others leverage.

Regardless of which path you choose, knowledge leverage is a strategic way to reduce risk and increase return to accelerate your wealth growth.

EXERCISE 1: LEARN SOMETHING NEW EVERY DAY

This is really more about adopting a habit (or process) than completing an exercise (or task).

It applies to knowledge leverage and it's very, very simple.

Learn something new every day!

Make it a habit. Become inquisitive. Be a student of your profession, no matter how advanced your skills, because one idea can change everything.

When you feed your mind every day with new knowledge and experience, you will become the go-to expert in very short order. In fact, in some professions, this can occur in just a year or two; and that's because the habit of perpetual growth through constant learning is so *rare*.

When you adopt this habit in your profession, it will lift your knowledge to rarefied territory, making your skill set so good that others can't ignore it. This will give you pricing and negotiating power, resulting in a higher income for your wealth plan.

Commit to learning something new every day.

EXERCISE 2: WHAT IS YOUR COMPETITIVE ADVANTAGE?

What specialized knowledge and experience do you already have, or can you develop?

Think about how you can convert that specialized knowledge or experience into a competitive business advantage by listing your talents/interests and matching them with a list of opportunities.

- What problems can you solve with that knowledge or experience that people or businesses would gladly pay for?

- How could you expand your knowledge and experience to increase your competitive advantage so your services are even more valuable?

Now reverse the process and also identify the areas where you have *no* competitive advantage, or possibly even a competitive *disadvantage*. You want to become equally clear about the areas where you have no edge, so you can define your business plan in a way that maximizes your strengths and minimizes your weaknesses.

You want to know where to go, and what to avoid or manage around. Both are helpful as you develop your wealth plan.

Always remember that your *talent* never limits you. What holds you back is a limited vision of the opportunities that match your talent.

IMPLEMENTATION

PUTTING IT ALL INTO PRACTICE TO ACHIEVE FINANCIAL FREEDOM

THE FIRST RULE OF ANY TECHNOLOGY USED IN BUSINESS IS THAT AUTOMATION APPLIED TO AN EFFICIENT OPERATION WILL MAGNIFY THE EFFICIENCY. THE SECOND IS THAT AUTOMATION APPLIED TO AN INEFFICIENT OPERATION WILL MAGNIFY THE INEFFICIENCY.

– BILL GATES

If you feel a little overwhelmed by all the choices for applying leverage, you're not alone.

I've spent an adult lifetime gathering the ideas in this book into usable form and putting them into practice. I then deepened my learning by coaching others for two decades on how to do the same.

Nobody is born with these skills; they can only be learned through careful application.

EFFICIENCY FIRST, LEVERAGE SECOND

The starting point is to realize that there's a right and a wrong way to apply leverage. This is critically important because one approach will make you rich and the other will make a mess of your finances.

Always remember that leverage is just an accelerator for whatever business process is already in place. It's not a magic pill for whatever ails your finances.

When you multiply an efficient operation through leverage, you increase profits. Conversely, when you leverage an inefficient operation, you multiply the losses. Leverage won't convert a losing business model into a winner unless significant efficiencies are gained from increased scale. Otherwise, leverage will just multiply what's already there.

Financial leverage only makes sense when the return on investment capital exceeds the interest cost of capital. It's a simple rule, but many forget it and end up leveraging results that aren't already profitable. That's a mistake.

And when you delegate work using time leverage, the return on employee productivity must be greater than what the employee costs you; otherwise, you're just magnifying a losing proposition.

The same rule applies to technology automation or any other form of leverage in this course. It must already be efficient and profitable, because leverage will simply magnify what's already there.

With that in mind, the first rule is to always *maximize* the efficiency of your business process *before* you multiply it with leverage. Additionally, it must already be profitable, or made profitable through scale; otherwise, leverage won't help you.

You must pay the price upfront to raise your business to profitability. Only then do you introduce leverage to overcome the wall to future growth caused by resource constraints. That's when you bring in leverage to expand those resources, blow through those constraints, and multiply your growth.

Remember, it always starts with building a profitable, efficient business model. That has to come first. Leverage will not solve profitability problems or business inefficiencies.

Think of it in two stages. The first stage is getting your business to profitability so that scaling growth through leverage makes business sense. The second stage is identifying the constraints holding you back from that greater growth so you can leverage your way through those barriers.

A COMPLETE TIMELINE FOR APPLYING LEVERAGE IN ANY BUSINESS

There's a natural progression to growing your business and applying leverage.

1. **Prove the Model** – In the beginning, your business absorbs all your time to get it rolling. That's why business often seems hard at first; it requires a lot of effort to persist through the learning curve, figure it all out, and turn a prof-

it. You know you're at this stage of development because you're working long hours, learning rapidly, and as soon as you stop putting in your time, the income will stop.

2. **Improve Profitability** – After you've bootstrapped the process at a small scale to fully prove out your model, the next step is leveraging it up with any of the six types of leverage to grow profits. That means streamlining all operations into a tight, efficient business process that minimizes costs and maximizes revenues.

   Please notice that I use the term "business" in this discussion, but all of these rules are equally true for running a paper asset investment process or a real estate investment project. You want to master the model at a small scale to honor risk management principles before you leverage it up to multiply results. The key idea is to always fail on a small scale so that you minimize the inevitable losses that occur during the learning curve, and then scale up with leverage after it's fully proven.

3. **Create Business Systems** – The next step is to convert all the business knowledge you have developed into systems so *they* can run everything instead of *you*. You might still be doing the work, or maybe you have an assistant, but the systems (or standard operating procedures) are

what govern how things get done. It's no longer about your knowledge because you've replaced yourself with systems.

4.   **Hire and Delegate** – This is the business development stage where you begin the process of eliminating yourself from the production equation. This makes freedom possible and converts the business into an *asset*, instead of just a job where you are self-employed. This also opens the door to overcoming skill constraints that hold your business growth back because you're hiring people with specialized expertise. As the business continues to grow, it then becomes cost-efficient to leverage other people's knowledge by building a team of legal, accounting, and other specialty advisors. Your goal is to hire the smartest people in each specialty to multiply the knowledge that runs your business.

Eventually you reach the point where you're red-lining the number of hours you can put into the business and bumping up against a ceiling of constraints. That's when it makes sense to overcome those constraints to growth by applying the appropriate leverage tools using the following rules.

1.   The first rule is to be open to new ways to streamline your business processes even further. Just because you always did it one way at a prior stage of business development doesn't mean

there's not a better way to do it as you expand. Your management and production processes will change with growth because the knowledge that got you where you are isn't what's going to jump you to the next level. Be willing to step outside the box of tradition, where "that's the way it's always been done" runs things, by looking for ways to reinvent your processes for greater efficiency at each level of growth.

2.   The second rule is to create synergy by layering systems to multiply the impact. Find the interconnectedness between your business systems and products to gain exponential increases in profit and growth that are greater than the sum of their parts.

For example, my working at a hedge fund to master investing connected my financial goal to become a skilled investor with my need to make a buck and support myself. It was a multi-layered, highly leveraged strategy where I got paid handsomely to develop the skills I wanted anyway and would have gladly paid to learn.

Another example is how all my educational products serve a single customer need (achieving financial freedom), so that all products relate to each other in a single sales funnel that creates back-end sales, thus increasing the lifetime value of each customer. The idea is to look for multiple points of leverage in your plans so that 2+2=7.

3. The final rule is to value differences and take advantage of them. Your strengths will be different from the next person's strengths. Know what you're good at and maximize that asset. Once you've done that, then do the opposite by identifying those personal *deficiencies* that cause constraints to your growth – so you can overcome them with leverage. Your expertise will compliment another person's different expertise. Seek out those differences and leverage them to your advantage.

For example, in my business I don't touch technology or design. Instead, I have a specialized team of experts that live and breathe those two subjects as their sole expertise. They can't do what I do, and I can't do what they do. Their highly specialized skills complement mine so that together we accomplish more.

USING LEVERAGE TO LEVERAGE LEVERAGE

As you become more adept at applying leverage, you'll begin to see how one type of leverage connects or bleeds into the others.

For example, you could argue that I'm leveraging my wealth to buy me enough time to build Financial

Mentor, that leverages my knowledge into products using technology, so I can hire employees to do all the tasks I don't know how to do, so I can acquire capital to leverage in real estate with mortgage financing that will then be leveraged into…

I could go on, but you get the picture… it's like one of those nested Russian dolls with a doll inside a doll inside a doll.

Another example is how franchising is a combination of systems leverage, time leverage, and knowledge leverage. Ultimately they're selling a business system with training that's based on knowing what's proven to work, which then leverages the time of each franchisee through fees back to the franchisor.

This book is one part knowledge leverage, one part systems leverage, one part marketing leverage, one part technology leverage, and one part time leverage. But how can you separate the time leverage and the knowledge leverage? One couldn't exist without the other. The same is true with the systems and marketing leverage. In fact, this book couldn't exist if any one component of leverage *failed*.

The point is: all six types of leverage work synergistically together. They are not mutually exclusive. Each is a tool in your toolbox that has its proper use in the right situation to remove a specific constraint to growth, and when the tools are applied together, they produce a compound effect.

In addition, there's a correct process for implementing leverage in your wealth plan, where you first prove the business model on a small scale, as previously described, before you leverage that model up to multiply your results.

This makes leverage both a science and an art form. In other words, the principles are scientific, but the creative application of those principles to your wealth plan is an art form. That's what makes building wealth creative and fun!

So the relevant question to consider is: What proportion of your day are you spending applying the leverage tools available to you? Specifically, ask yourself:

- How many points of leverage does my wealth plan include?

- What are all the ways that I'm actively applying leverage on a weekly basis right now?

- How many new leverage strategies will I integrate into my wealth plan this year?

Nobody gets rich without leverage. If you aren't employing leverage in your business and wealth plans, you're compromising the speed, time, and work effort necessary to reach each level of success.

If you aren't using leverage, you're working harder than you should, to earn less than you could, and that isn't going to make you wealthy.

START SOMEWHERE

You don't need to master every form of leverage to succeed. You don't even need to master the *majority* of the leverage strategies.

Sure, the more you master leverage, the greater results you'll be able to produce, with fewer of your own resources. But I've never worked with a coaching client who mastered all six types of leverage. Everyone has a weak spot… you and I included.

Or said differently, we all have natural strengths that we tend toward, so it's highly unlikely you'll be naturally strong in every type of leverage. Instead, you'll gravitate toward certain types of leverage while avoiding (or overlooking) other types of leverage.

The good news is: That's okay! You only need enough leverage to get the job done. Results are what matters.

ENOUGH LEVERAGE TO GET THE JOB DONE

*

| 1 | Network & Relationship Leverage (Reclusive - Less Comfortable With) | 10 |

*

| 1 | Systems Leverage - Natural | 10 |

For example, I would rate myself as a 2 on a 1-to-10 scale for using network and relationship leverage in my business; whereas I'm a 9 or 10 for using systems leverage. I naturally think in terms of business systems, but I'm a bit reclusive so networks and relationships are something I'm less comfortable with and have to work at. It's not a natural part of my being.

The reason I share my own leverage weak points is so you don't have to stress or feel incompetent if you don't work all forms of leverage from the start. It's okay, and it's actually common.

I started with systems leverage because it was my natural strong suit. I fell into financial leverage through my investment management business with no intention whatsoever; I just fumbled into it. I then *fought* my perfectionist tendencies and my need to do everything myself, in order to painstakingly add time leverage – exactly in the order I taught it to you in that chapter. Slowly but surely, the entire leverage framework came together exactly as you see it in this book.

But the point is that success came through the application of *small parts* of this entire leverage framework because it's so powerful that you only need what's absolutely necessary. *Don't worry* about what you haven't achieved; just focus on the constraints in front of you that limit your growth and apply the correct leverage tool for that situation. Over time, you'll master more and more of the tools until progressively the entire framework becomes second nature.

But in the meantime you have to start somewhere....

The main thing is: don't be overwhelmed by all the information in this book. Instead, pick a few leverage strategies that excite you the most, and don't worry about the others. Because they're all interconnected, you'll find that the more you work with them, the more types of leverage you'll naturally include in your plans without any additional stress or worry.

Again, just pick an obvious starting point for your plan and *take action*. As long as you've got enough leverage in your wealth plan to achieve your goals, it's not a problem if other forms of leverage are ignored.

With that said, obviously the more leverage you can successfully include in your plans, the better. But it's more important to just get started rather than risk getting overwhelmed by perfectionism that causes you to do nothing. Instead, just move forward as best you can with whatever works for you now, and commit to constant improvement over time.

Imperfect action is better than no action, and when coupled with constant improvement, you'll master far more than you thought possible in far less time than you imagined.

Your instruction on leverage is now complete. I hope

everything you've learned helps you achieve greater financial results, in less time than you imagined possible, and puts you on the path to early financial independence with greater security for you and your loved ones.

If you have taken the chapter on Knowledge and Experience to heart, and are ready to dive deeper into the strategies I teach, you may want to start with my training on risk management. This is a video course available at financialmentor.com/educational-products/risk-management-course.

If reading is more your thing, I have additional books available for purchase on my website or on Amazon.com. I recommend *How Much Money Do I Need To Retire?*, financialmentor.com/educational-products/ebooks/how-much-money-do-i-need-to-retire which takes you beyond the scientific façade of conventional retirement planning with refreshingly straightforward, easy-to-understand, and concise advice on how to retire wealthy.

No matter which path you take to further your education, please remember that building wealth is *an adventure in personal growth*. The money is just the carrot. Who you become through the process is what really matters. I hope you enjoy the adventure!

Todd Tresidder
www.financialmentor.com

QUICK REFERENCE

OVERVIEW

Accumulating wealth comes from compound growth of personal capital and financial capital over time. The advantage of using leverage is it doesn't have to be your personal capital or financial capital. That's a game-changing difference.

Leverage allows you to separate your wealth growth from your return on equity equation, and it allows you to break the connection between your income and hours worked. Breaking these connections opens the possibility for entirely different financial strategies that can radically increase your income and grow your wealth while actually working less.

Leverage releases you from the limitations of conventional financial planning built around working a job, earning money, then saving what's left over at the end of the month so you can invest in a conventional asset allocation portfolio of paper assets. This is a slow, low-leverage path to wealth accumulation, usually taking a lifetime to acquire financial security (unless you pursue extreme frugality).

The leveraged path opens up accelerated strategies using

other people's resources so that your wealth growth isn't limited by your own time, money, skills, and abilities. These added resources are what frees your wealth growth from the return on equity limitations and your income growth from time-for-money limitations.

But it gets even better because leverage is also the tool you'll use to overcome the obstacles that hold you back from greater success. Nearly every obstacle you face and roadblock standing in your way is overcome by one of the six types of leverage.

In other words, leverage is both a tool for accelerating your wealth growth, and it's a tool for breaking through the constraints that limit your success. Best of all, it doesn't have to be risky because only financial leverage both increases risk and return. The other forms of leverage can accelerate your results while reducing risk at the same time, giving you the best of both worlds.

In short, you either learn to master leverage or you'll work far harder than necessary to produce far fewer results than you're capable of.

PRINCIPLES: THE 9 PRINCIPLES OF LEVERAGE

1. **Mathematical Expectancy:** Your wealth compounds according to mathematical expectancy, which is probability times payoff. Smart wealth builders tilt the payoff portion of the equation utilizing both leverage (to maximize gains) and

risk management (to control losses). Skilled payoff management produces the counterintuitive result that you can be wrong nine times out of 10 and still achieve extraordinary wealth. Another advantage of payoff management is it's within your control; whereas, probability is not because it's dependent on an unknowable future.

2. **Reciprocal Exchange:** Trading your time for money, or trading your money for a product or fixed interest rate of return provides a limited payoff, which limits your wealth growth. The constraint is your own personal resources because that's all you have to exchange. The solution is to shift your strategy from the reciprocal exchange model where you trade *time* for dollars, to trading *value* for dollars – because value can be provided in many different ways using leverage that frees you from personal resource limitations.

3. **Opportunity Costs:** Your personal resources of time and money are limited resulting in opportunity costs. Whatever you choose to spend time and money on means it cannot be spent elsewhere. Eventually your financial growth hits a wall because you can't trade any more time to produce any more money when you're already working as much as you can tolerate. The only way to overcome your personal opportunity cost

limitation is to leverage other people's resources so you can tilt the payoff portion of the expectancy equation.

4. **Time Freedom:** The fact that time is limited is what makes financial acceleration through leverage so incredibly important. Leverage is how you buy back your time by achieving financial freedom faster, so less of your life is spent on money pursuits. If you want to know how long it will take you to become financially independent, just look at how much of your limited time is spent in reciprocal exchange versus leveraged growth.

5. **Give Value and Solve Problems:** Business is about solving problems – because people will gladly pay to leverage your solution to their problems. Your goal is to grow beyond the reciprocal exchange mindset by figuring out ways to use leverage to create more value and solve more problems. When you master this skill, your growing wealth becomes a measure of how much value you've given to others.

6. **Make Yourself Unnecessary:** As you pursue financial independence don't try to be a super-hero and do it all yourself. If your goals are wealth and freedom, then the only way you can have both together is with the help of others. There's always more to do than any one person can do so focus your limited time on just the

highest value activities requiring your attention. Then delegate or partner so someone else can do the rest. This achieves more, better, faster results and also frees up your time and energy to focus on your highest leverage strengths.

7. **Upfront Costs, Benefits Lag:** Leverage seldom results in instant gratification. There is always an upfront cost that must be paid in terms of time, training, or system development before you can benefit from the lagged results that will be produced. That's why wealth growth is the habit of delayed gratification.

8. **Expand the Gap:** Your objective for all leveraged growth and risk management strategies is to expand the gap between how much you earn versus how much you spend, thus resulting in equity growth. In the traditional model, that equity growth translates through savings over time to become investment capital; whereas, in non-traditional assets like business and real estate, your equity grows geometrically as a multiple of the increased earnings without regard to savings or time limitations.

9. **Financial Independence:** Mastering leverage leads to financial freedom which gives you back your time, the ultimate scarce resource. More time opens up more possibilities to embrace the adventure of life and live it fully, which is the real objective.

STRATEGIES: THE 6 TYPES OF LEVERAGE

FINANCIAL LEVERAGE — UTILIZE OTHER PEOPLE'S MONEY SO YOU'RE NOT LIMITED TO YOUR OWN NET WORTH

Financial leverage comes in three different forms: (1) borrowed money, (2) contractual leverage, (3) and operating leverage. It's a valuable tool for your wealth plan because it eliminates any excuse for money being an obstacle to your financial growth.

However, financial leverage is the one type that both increases potential rewards and decreases the odds of survivability. It makes the good times great, and the bad times unbearable. That's why the following risk management guidelines are essential for financial leverage.

1. Don't over-leverage because the best plans will still experience temporary setbacks, at a minimum. Sometimes worse.

2. Always have an exit strategy to remove leverage and preserve equity so you're prepared with clear action steps should adversity strike.

3. Only leverage assets that provide positive cash flow net of debt service and expenses.

4. Avoid using financial leverage when the income stream supporting the assets is volatile.

5. Financial leverage is most appropriate when your goal is maximum wealth growth, but

is inappropriate when your goal is security and stability.

6.   Avoid financial leverage in deflationary economic environments.

TIME LEVERAGE — EMPLOY OTHER PEOPLE'S TIME SO YOU'RE NOT LIMITED TO 24 HOURS IN A DAY

Time is your ultimate scarce resource. The fact that you can't save it or create more of it is why leverage strategies to accelerate your financial freedom are important. It's how you recover your limited time from being spent on unsatisfying drudgery.

The goal of time leverage is to release your income growth from the boundaries of time, and to get more stuff done without using any of your time. You achieve these two goals through a progressive four-step process:

1.   The first step is to increase the proportion of truly productive time in your day. You want to recover those marginal hours that will literally double and triple your total productivity.

2.   The next step is to delegate projects so you can multiply the amount of time working toward your goals, thus accelerating your progress.

3.   Next, increase your time leverage from linear project leverage to the more valuable process leverage. Identify all repeating functions in your

business that don't need your active involvement and delegate them.

4.   Finally, you can further increase leverage by replacing human time from the production equation with scalable business system automation using technology and systems leverage.

The goal is to get more work done so you can create more profit while working less.

TECHNOLOGY AND SYSTEMS LEVERAGE – SET UP A SCALABLE MODEL ONCE SO THE SYSTEMS CAN DO THE WORK THOUSANDS OF TIMES

If your goal is to own your business (rather than letting it own you) then you need to remove yourself from the production process. Convert all activities required to run your business into scalable, efficient systems that aren't dependent on any individual.

1.   The starting point is to process map repetitive tasks into standard operating procedures so that reliable, high-quality, efficient results are produced every time with a minimum of mistakes.

2.   The next step is to integrate technology leverage so that you start replacing human labor with machine labor, further reducing costs and improving results.

3.   Finally, design audit controls with checks and balances into your systems so they're self-correcting.

It costs time and money to get systems leverage working for you, but those resources are well spent because the result is greater wealth, less risk, and more freedom. And that's a goal well worth pursuing.

COMMUNICATIONS AND MARKETING LEVERAGE — ACCESS OTHER PEOPLE'S AUDIENCES THROUGH MAGAZINES, NEWSLETTERS, AND DATABASES SO YOU CAN COMMUNICATE WITH MILLIONS FOR THE SAME EFFORT AS ONE

Communications leverage is the bridge that creates marketing leverage out of networks. It has three main advantages:

1.   Low marginal cost for each touch point because it's generally priced as a fixed expense allowing you to cost-effectively increase the frequency and breadth of communication.

2.   Builds brand loyalty and trust by using technology to cost effectively deliver value through articles, courses, videos, and other educational resources.

3.   Gives immediate data feedback so you can test offers in minutes at minimal cost then correct and adjust messaging until the conversion rate proves cost-effectiveness.

There are many tactics to increase communications leverage (upsell, cross-sell, referral systems, joint ventures, automated sales funnels, continuity sales programs, media outreach), but they all boil down to two objectives.

1. Find new customers.

2. Increase the lifetime value of existing customers.

The key to success in communications leverage is knowing how to cut through all the information noise with a meaningful message that serves your customers. Give them something valuable so you're not just adding to all the noise that already clutters their lives.

NETWORK AND RELATIONSHIP LEVERAGE — EMPLOY OTHER PEOPLE'S CONNECTIONS AND RESOURCES SO YOU'RE NOT LIMITED TO YOUR OWN

Network leverage is based on relationships that exchange value instead of money. The value exchanged might include contacts, resources, strategies, experiences, referrals, support, or any other form of value that costs the giver nothing but makes a big difference for the receiver.

The reason relationship leverage is important is because the root of all business is human relationship. When you know how to leverage those relationships ethically, you'll create more business, faster, with less risk, and with less of your own resources.

The four steps to building a network that multiplies your wealth are:

1. Decide who you want in your network.

2. Connect with those people.

3. Build the relationship over time by giving and paying it forward – never using. Be the first to offer up your contacts and resources before making any demands on the relationship. Play the long game.

4. Finally, when the time is right, you can ask for an appropriate level of help.

Building a strong professional network of strategic contacts is something that can take years. It requires effort, but strategic alliances with the right people can make or break your wealth plan. The key is who you know, what you know, and how you ethically apply those resources.

KNOWLEDGE AND EXPERIENCE LEVERAGE – UTILIZE OTHER PEOPLE'S EXPERTISE, OR LEVERAGE YOUR OWN EXPERTISE

Knowledge is the foundation of all wealth-generating processes because it converts resources into something with economic value. Stated another way, physical capital owes most of its value to intellectual capital.

Unfortunately, the ability to learn and grow intellectual capital is limited by your time and ability to internalize information. There's always more to learn than time to learn it.

That's why hiring an expert who lives and breathes the knowledge you require can be such an effective leverage strategy to save you time and accelerate your wealth.

Alternatively, if your goal is to increase your earning capacity, it might make sense to gather the knowledge yourself so as to become the go-to expert that others leverage.

Regardless of which path you choose, knowledge leverage is a strategic way to reduce risk and increase return to accelerate your wealth growth.

IMPLEMENTATION

Nobody is born with leverage skills so don't get overwhelmed if these leverage strategies felt foreign or unusual. The good news is there's a strategic way to implement leverage, regardless of your current skill level, that will best capitalize on your existing strengths and minimize any weaknesses.

The first point to remember is leverage is just an accelerator for whatever business process is already in place. When you multiply an efficient operation through leverage, you increase profits. Conversely, when you leverage an inefficient operation, you multiply losses.

So the first rule is: bootstrap your way to profitability so that you control for risk of loss before ever applying leverage. Think of it in two stages.

- The first stage is controlling risk to minimize losses while developing a profitable model.

- The second stage is multiplying that profitable model with leverage to create a huge win that tilts the payoff portion of your expectancy equation.

The second rule is: all six types of leverage work synergistically together. They are not mutually exclusive. Each type provides a unique tool for removing a specific constraint to growth, and when the tools are applied together, they produce a compound effect. So just start with whatever leverage tool is most immediately appealing and don't worry about the rest because they'll naturally fit into your wealth plan in the fullness of time.

The goal is to accelerate your wealth growth and save your time because if you aren't using leverage then you're working harder than you should, to earn less than you could.

BONUS CONTENT

This book has been about taking action, so I encourage you to take action now. To make it easy we've provided a complete set of printable templates, forms, and reference guides to help you, completely free of charge. It includes:

- 2 sample Standard Operating Procedures
- 101+ Leverage Hacks
- A Printable Exercise Workbook
- And an accountability chart for implementation

You can get immediate access to all of these resources at: https://financialmentor.com/free-stuff/leverage-book.

ACKNOWLEDGEMENTS

First, I need to thank Erin Millard, my assistant. The rule is to always hire people better than yourself. Erin defines that rule. Without her constant support, this book wouldn't be in your hands right now.

Second, I'd like to acknowledge Julie Broad and her professional publishing team at Book Launchers. Their support and assistance with editing and designing took my rough draft and polished it into the book you hold today.

Finally, I'd like to acknowledge you, the reader. It is your passion for learning that feeds my passion for teaching. Thank you.

ABOUT THE AUTHOR

 Todd R. Tresidder's financial writing has been featured in the Wall Street Journal, Smart Money Magazine, Investor's Business Daily, Forbes, Yahoo Finance, Inc., USA Today, and more. He is a former hedge fund manager who "retired" at age 35 to become a financial consumer advocate and money coach. In his spare time he's an outdoor recreational enthusiast with varied interests from backpacking and adventure travel to endurance running and cycling. He writes nine months of the year from his home in Reno, Nevada while his kids are in school, and he plays the rest of the year. You can learn more about Todd at financialmentor.com.

ADDITIONAL BOOKS BY TODD TRESIDDER

How Much Money Do I Need To Retire?

Don't Hire A Financial Coach! (Until You Read This Book)

The 4% Rule and Safe Withdrawal Rates in Retirement

Variable Annuity Pros and Cons:
Surprising Truths Your Advisor Won't Tell You

Investment Fraud:
How Financial "Experts" Rip You Off
and What To Do About It

ADDITIONAL COURSES BY TODD TRESIDDER

This book was created from just three lessons taken from my master course, Expectancy Wealth Planning. If you like this book, then you'll love the full course.

Expectancy Wealth Planning can be found at financialmentor.com/educational-products/expectancy-wealth-plan.